OF ORCHIDS

JÖRN PINSKE

THE MACMILLAN BOOK

OF ORCHIDS

Translated by Carole Ottesen

COLLIER BOOKS
MACMILLAN PUBLISHING COMPANY
New York

COLLIER MACMILLAN PUBLISHERS
London

Macmillan Publishing Company
866 Third Avenue, New York, N.Y. 10022
Collier Macmillan Canada, Inc.

Title of the original German edition:
ORCHIDEEN FÜR ZU HAUSE
© 1984 BLV Verlagsgesellschaft mbH,
München

English translation copyright © 1986 by
Macmillan Publishing Company,
a division of Macmillan, Inc.

Library of Congress Cataloging-
in-Publication Data
Pinske, Jörn.
    The Macmillan book of orchids.

    Translation of: Orchideen für zu Hause.
    Includes index.
    1. Orchid culture.   2. Orchids.   I. Title
SB409.P5613 1986   635.9'3415   85-28058
ISBN 0-02-063520-6

Macmillan books are available at special
discounts for bulk purchases for sales
promotions, premiums, fund-raising, or
educational use.

For details, contact:

Special Sales Director
Macmillan Publishing Company
866 Third Avenue
New York, N.Y. 10022

10 9 8 7 6 5 4 3 2 1

Printed in Germany

Contents

Introduction

If the queen of flowers is the rose, surely the empress is to be found among the orchids—and the beggars there as well. Orchids aren't only big-blossomed, exotic beauties from the tropics, they are also small, nondescript plants that grow in northern meadows. Certainly they are no longer a rarity. In 1982, at the biggest flower show ever held in the Netherlands, there were nearly 230 million orchid flowers, and another 583,960 potted orchids. Nearly all were sold, but only a very few of those who bought these orchids realized that their purchases were the result of four or more years of cultivation. Of the many orchids sold at the show, how many are still alive today? Do orchids, in fact, become throwaway plants before they even have the chance to become house plants? Or is it perhaps the orchid's fault that it simply isn't destined to be a houseplant?

Actually, tropical orchids do make good houseplants—but not without correct information and, above all, patience. Here's the information; the patience is up to you.

Vanda coerulea, known for its rare blue flower color. Deep blue varieties have already been found.

Introducing Orchids

Introducing Orchids

Most people will first make the acquaintance of an orchid at the florist. There, among the cut flowers, orchids are no longer the rarity they once were. Their durability is renowned; their exotic appearance and rich color combinations make them precious—a "precious" that is no longer indicative of price. Over the past few years, orchids have become much more economical and available—although potted varieties still are found only seldomly in florist shops. Yet they have nonetheless retained their aura of "exotic and exclusive" along with the notion of their tropical origin. As stated earlier, they don't all come from the tropics, and a few even grow in our own climate, but their existence is threatened by industrial land use. Why orchids may function as barometers of environmental pollution will be easy to understand as you proceed in this book.

Origin of Orchids

If there was once a geographical cradle of orchid life, it hasn't yet been ascertained, and there are only hypotheses. However, we do know that there were orchids at the beginning of the Cenozoic era (60 million years ago) in tropical Asia and America, and that the most primitive forms today are found in the area of the Malaysian archipelago. Thus, many experts consider this location the original home of the orchid.

For those of us who want to grow orchids, their origin is of less importance. What is amazing is their distribution on the earth. Orchids are found in Scandinavia, Siberia, Canada, Patagonia, South Africa, Tasmania, and New Zealand. Their adaptability is beyond belief, and it is this very characteristic that makes them ideal for home cultivation. Scarcely any other family of plants adapts as well to the not-always-optimum conditions of the average home as do orchids, with so little attention given to their requirements.

Actually, the idea of their tropical origin is not just a stereotype: 90 percent of the 25,000 known species come from tropical areas, where they are found in different types of highlands. They are subdivided into 750 genera.

Cypripedium calceolus, our native lady's slipper. Unlike the tropical species (*Paphiopedilum*), it is not suitable for home culture. Grow in the garden in semishade in a rich sweet soil.

Introducing Orchids

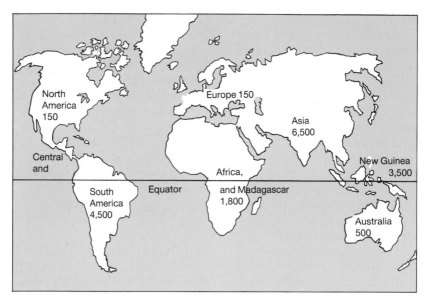

Geographic distribution of orchids, with approximate numbers of species. Most species grow in the tropics. Heavy concentrations are found in Asia and South America.

Scientific Nomenclature

Like all other plants—and animals, too—orchids have scientific names. This fact is important for anyone who deals with plants. The local or common name won't necessarily be understood elsewhere, or its designation can lead to hopeless confusion. For example, one of the best-known room orchids is—first, the correct name—*Rossioglossum grande* (Lindl.) Garey et Kennedy—better known as *Odontoglossum grande.* The name is a combination of the genus (*Rossioglossum*), the species name (*grande,* not capitalized), and the name of the first person(s) to describe it (Lindl., Garey, and Kennedy). Lindl. is an abbreviation of the name of the first person to describe this orchid, in this case John Lindley (1799–1865), a professor of botany. The plant was identified by its genus name, *Odontoglossum.* But in 1976 botanists Garey and Kennedy changed the name *Odontoglossum,* in the interest of clarifying botanical categories, and added on another genus, *Rossioglossum,* and this new name was accepted internationally. The old

Odontoglossum (*Rossioglossum*) *grande,* one of the most beautiful orchid species for cool to temperate rooms—not suitable for warm rooms.

Odontoglossum was now desig-
nated a synonym and Lindley's
name was set in parentheses.
It all sounds complicated, but it
does provide a means of giving
plants names that will be understood anywhere in the world. A
common name like "tiger orchid"
won't be understood outside the
United States, let alone from state
to state (or region to region) where
the very same plant has another
"common" name—"spotted
orchid," perhaps.
But don't be alarmed. Once you
look over the system of scientific
nomenclature, you'll quickly get
used to the names. In most
horticultural usage, the names
of those who first described
the plants are not included,
and for reasons of simplifica-
tion, this book won't use them
either.

Introducing Orchids

Nomenclature of Cultivated Orchids

The nomenclature of orchid cultivars was established by *Sander's List of Orchid Hybrids* in 1906, and is now maintained by the Royal Horticultural Society in London. All orchid hybrids are registered with the society and published in editions of Sander's list.

Today there are almost twice as many hybrids listed as there are natural species (25,000). Hybrids also make up the main body of those grown by orchid hobbyists. This is why it is important to be immediately able to recognize a plant as a hybrid. The international rules of nomenclature are also valid for orchids. Among the hybrids, one distinguishes:

1. Species hybrid. For example: *Odontoglossum crispum* × *Odontoglossum triumphans.* The cross between these two species of one genus keeps the genus name, but acquires a new grex name (*grex* is Latin for herd, swarm), which begins with a capital; here, *Odontoglossum* Harvengtense, a natural hybrid.

2. Genus hybrid. This type of hybrid acquires an "artificial" name made from parts of the genera, or a completely new name, that has to end in "era."

Genus hybrid *Brassolae-liocattleya,* cultivar 'Stilles Gedenken.'

For example:
Cattleya trianae × *Laelia perrinii* = *Laeliocattleya* Bambino.

Sander's List of Orchid Hybrids tells us the parents of each cross, the hybridizer, and the date of the cross. Sometimes three genera are used in a cross, and the names may be put together: *Cattleya* × *Laelia* × *Brassavola* = *Brassolaeliocattleya.* These combined names are independent of the order of crossing. Sometimes these awkward combinations are simplified when an entirely new name ending in "era" is formed. An example is: *Cochlioda* × *Miltonia* × *Odontoglossum* is called *Vuylstekeara,* after Belgian hybridizer Vuylsteke.

Let's keep this particular example because the *Vuylstekeara* will soon be a common term for every orchid lover. *Vuylstekeara* Cambria is one of the best-known orchids for the home. We know that the genera *Cochlioda, Miltonia,* and *Odontoglossum* were involved in this cross. The capitalization of the name "Cambria" immediately tells us that we are dealing with a hybrid. In addition, one often finds a cultivar name in single quotes: *Vuylstekeara* Cambria 'Plush.' 'Plush' is the cultivar or variety name. With orchids, these names are only used with clones or vegetatively propagated plants. As already mentioned, all names must be registered in London if they wish international recognition, and in the chapter on orchid propagation we will touch again on this matter.

Flower Characteristics

The flower of an orchid is similar to that of a lily. Some lilies are even mistaken for orchids, such as the *Gloriosa rothschildiana*. The diagram of an orchid blossom essentially reveals the same underlying structure as that of the lily. One finds five rings of three: an outer and an inner ring of petals, as well as a ring of stamens and the reproductive parts. With the orchid, as pictured in the diagram, there is a reduction in the number of stamens, which fuse with the pistil

Different varieties of the hybrid *Vuylstekeara* Cambria: *left* 'Wichmanns Favorit,' *center* 'Plush,' *right* 'Lensings Favorit.'

Introducing Orchids

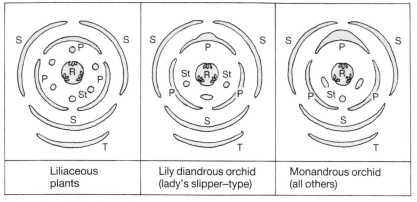

Liliaceous plants	Lily diandrous orchid (lady's slipper–type)	Monandrous orchid (all others)

A comparison of three flower diagrams.
T = torus   P = petals   S = sepals   St = stamen   R = reproductive parts

to form a special organ, the column. It is the column that is the distinguishing feature of an orchid. Aspects of flower structure mentioned below are the clearly apparent, external details:

1. The diandrous flower has two more fertile stamens.
2. The monandrous, the majority of orchids, has only one fertile stamen.

The *Cypripedioideae* is an important group for indoor gardeners to which belongs the genus *Paphiopedilum,* the lady's slipper.
A hallmark of this group is the slipper-shaped "lip," which, together with petals on either side, belongs to the corolla, the inner ring. The outer ring, the calyx, consists of

three sepals. The top sepal, called the "fan" in lady's slipper, always arches backward in opposition to the two lower sepals—grown together—behind the "slipper." (See illustration.)
In monandrous orchids, the lip is the most distinguishing feature. Either funnel- or tube-shaped, it stands out because of its color and shape.
The lip is one of the petals but is clearly different from the identical lateral pair, set slightly behind. The central sepal may or may not resemble the lower pair.

Introducing Orchids

In describing orchid blossoms we will always return to these basic features; therefore, it is worthwhile to learn what they are. Incidentally, the basic type of orchid flower is always a spike. The potential for multiple bloom is always there—even if only a single flower develops. For example, on the lady's slipper one can locate a latent bud, or with the *Paphiopedilum philippinense* more flowers actually develop.

When we speak of multiple blooming orchids, we always use the word "inflorescence"—even when the structure is really a raceme, corymb, or otherwise. Most often the flowers on the inflorescence open at very nearly the same time, although sometimes the lower (basal) flowers open first. Often the first blossom is long faded (especially in *Phalaenopsis* or *Oncidium kramerianum*), before the last bud unfolds. There is a widespread misconception that every orchid lasts indefinitely. A flower, and this is true not only of orchids, lasts as long as necessary—that is, long enough for fertilization to take place.

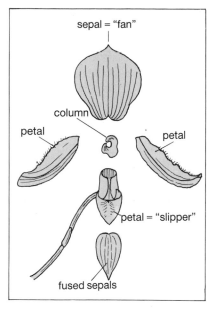

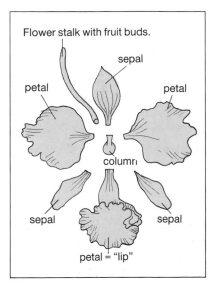

Structure of a diandrous (*above*) and a monandrous (*below*) orchid blossom.

Introducing Orchids

The flower has built-in help—one can almost call it advertisement—to make itself noticeable: its fragrance, color, size, and, not least of all, its long-lasting bloom. These advertisements appeal to a certain clientele—the agents of fertilization. Orchids are fertilized mainly by insects, but also by birds: 68 percent of orchids are fertilized by wasps, bees, and moths, and 12 percent are fertilized by mosquitoes, flies, and similar insects. Another 3 percent are fertilized by hummingbirds; 15 percent are visited by other animals, mainly insects (frequently ants); 2 percent of orchids are self-fertile (Brieger).

An agent of fertilization (here a hummingbird) at an orchid flower.

For orchid lovers—not the usual clientele—the exotic shapes of the flowers with their marvelous colors play the greatest role. Their remarkable durability is really a bonus. In *Phalaenopsis,* to cite one example, a flowering period of fifteen weeks or more is not uncommon.

The fragrance given off by an orchid enhances its appeal. Nevertheless, whether fragrance or stench is a matter of opinion. Some *Stanhopea* can cause headaches in sensitive individuals; the same reaction can occur with the *Oncidium ornithorhynchum,* the bird's-head orchid. But those who experience no pain find the scent sensual and lovely. Fortunately, everyone agrees that *Cattleya* and *Odontoglossum pulchellum* are both sweet-smelling flowers, affording only pleasant scents.

Aside from their flowers, orchids have two other unusual and closely related characteristics of the reproductive organs. First is the minute size of the seeds, called microsperm. The seed case contains no nourishment, unlike the apple seed that carries enough nourishment to allow for germination and the first stages of growth to occur without any outside help.

By the way, if you want to see a similar seed case, look in your kitchen; among the spices you'll surely find a vanilla bean, the seed case of the orchid *Vanilla planifolia.*

Of course it is greatly shrunken and discolored, but you'll still get a general idea.

A seed capsule like the vanilla bean holds a phenomenal number of seeds: 3,900,000 were once counted. Their weight was about 0.0003 mg; the average is about 0.0005 mg.

In order for such a small seed to germinate, it needs the help of special fungi.

Experts call these "symbiotic fungi". When we deal with orchid propagation, we'll come back to them. For home orchid culture, these fungi are really not important. The other characteristic of the or-

Ripe, open seed capsules of various orchids shown at approximately half scale.

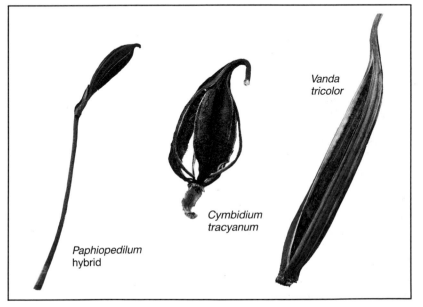

Vanda tricolor

Cymbidium tracyanum

Paphiopedilum hybrid

Introducing Orchids

chids is pollen dissemination. Unlike most pollen, which is carried by the wind, the orchids have prepackaged it, ready to be carried away by insects. These glued-together balls of pollen are called pollinia. The packaging makes it easier for the fertilizing agent to transfer large amounts of pollen to ensure fertilization.

Types of Growth

Because orchids hail from very different parts of the earth, they don't always look alike. Adaptation to a given environment will have caused the leaves, shoots, and roots to develop in different ways. There are two large and not always clearly distinguished types of growth. First is the so-called monopodial group, characterized by single-stem growth that increases indefinitely in height; there may or may not be side branches. The best-known examples are found among the genus *Vanda,* but *Phalaenopsis* is a monopodial orchid, too. The plant grows from the tip and may later lose its lower leaves.

In the second type, the sympodial orchids, there is limited stem growth. New growth, coming from a basal bud, extends the rhizome, forming a horizontal enlargement. This is the way that *Odontoglos-*

Vanda hybrid exhibiting typical monopodial growth.

sum and *Cattleya* grow. The way that orchids grow is important to consider in transplanting and also in propagation.

18

Pseudobulbs with new growth (*Catesetum*), longish form. The leaves of the sympodial *Dendrobium linguiforme* have taken on the shape and function of pseudobulbs.

not optimal for growth, sometimes through a resting period accompanied by drought or cold. Some orchids may even be called succulents (xerophytes).

Leaves

The varied leaf forms of orchids have adapted to the differing light conditions prevailing in the natural habitat. Some are almost succulent, others thin and flat. Sometimes they develop during a period of growth and will last for many years. At times it is difficult to tell the bulb from the leaf; other times they are clearly separate. Often colors, light to dark green, even brownish red, make the distinction

Pseudobulbs

One remarkable feature of many orchids is a thickening of the stem, called the pseudobulb. This thick growth serves as a reservoir for food and water. Pseudobulbs can be long, round, or oval in shape. Their presence indicates that climactic conditions over the course of the year in the orchid's natural habitat are variable. The plant has to overcome conditions

Introducing Orchids

easier. The function of these leaves, as with all green plants, is the same.

Roots

All plants grow from sound roots, whether ivy, rubber tree, or orchid. Maintaining and fostering root growth is the single most important cultivation practice.

A plant under cultivation, unlike those in the wild, has a very limited space at its disposal. If its roots are damaged, all the other organs suffer and the entire plant may die. It is the same with orchids, only they have a relatively limited root growth. Only during the orchid's period of active growth will the roots be active, and it is therefore very important when working with orchids to respect this period.

The root is the organ in orchids (as well as in other plants) that does the job of supplying water and minerals. Even a cursory glance reveals that orchids have relatively thick roots. A special layer of tissue surrounds the roots, the velamen, formed by dead tissue. This coating is filled with air and acts like a sponge, and these cells can quickly fill with water, a feature that maximizes the effect of brief rain showers or dew. For epiphytes (orchids that have left the ground), these roots are absolutely necessary. (See page 23.) Sometimes we speak of these as air roots. Special

Flattened anchoring roots on a freestanding log—air roots.

conductor cells located in the surface tissue allow moisture to be conducted from the surface of the roots to the inside.

Many epiphytes have roots so numerous and thickly branching that they build a nest of roots. Negative geotropism is what the experts call this phenomenon. Orchid leaves and plant parts are caught in the nest and provide nourishment as they decompose. An important feature of air roots is their ability to anchor the plant to a support. An anchor root needs to be both elastic enough to give with the wind yet secure enough to keep from loosening. For this reason, anchor roots flatten themselves against the underlying support. Terrestrial orchids, those

Air roots growing straight up appear to be building a nest.

growing on the ground, develop a coating of velamen on their roots; when this dies, root hairs take over the job of supplying water.

Fungi live in the velamen of roots and in certain parts of the roots. They also play a role in the germination of orchids. As fungi send out their threadlike hyphae, they augment the root system of the plant. Fungicides keep their activity limited to parts of the plants that benefit from their presence.

How Orchids Live

Most plants live with their roots in the earth, and so do native orchids. It seems obvious, but this fact isn't a hard and fast rule; only a few orchids really grow that way. These are called terrestrial orchids. Nearly 80 percent of tropical orchids (that is, 90 percent of all orchids) grow in another way: They leave the earth behind.

Why should orchids leave the security of the earth?

Imagine the plant world of the tropics, with its amazing variety of living things; it is beyond anything we know in our temperate climate. In the tropics there are hundreds of thousands of plants, all competing for light, and it is the orchid's tremendous adaptability that makes it possible for them to find an excellent solution to the light problem, by leaving the ground where competition among evergreen foliage of other trees and plants makes it too dark.

High up in the trees, generally in semishade, on branches—prefer-

Introducing Orchids

Introducing Orchids

An epiphytic plant community of orchids and bromeliads.

ably in the crotch of limbs—in the company of bromeliads and ferns, epiphytic orchids have found an ideal home. There, with the help of fungi, it is possible for ripe orchid seeds to germinate. Thus, great colonies of orchids originate. They are not parasites that bore into the flesh of the host plant, although once in a while they can damage a host. Damage can happen when orchids and other epiphytes become so numerous that they actually cause a tree or branch to topple.

The epiphytic way of life is the normal one for most orchids, especially those that we number among our houseplants. It is the grower's job to take this way of life into account.

For completeness' sake, a third orchid lifestyle, that of saprophytic orchids, is included here although they are not among those generally cultivated. Many other plant families include saprophytic members that live in symbiosis with fungi. Because they cannot produce much or any chlorophyll, they aren't green. Sometimes they don't even develop leaflike organs but grow scales instead. They acquire their nourishment, with the help of fungi, from dead organic material, and the fungus growth functions as their roots. Saprophytic orchids

Introducing Orchids

are found not only in the tropics but among native plants as well. For those who grow orchids at home, however, the terrestrial and epiphytic orchids are the important ones.

There are also numerous transitional forms, types of orchids that can live in either a terrestrial or epiphytic situation. These are particularly common among the lithophytes, plants that live on stones, which can be found growing on the ground or on the stones themselves.

Instructions for care will concentrate on the needs of terrestrial and epiphytic orchids. Among the typical epiphytes are *Cattleya, Phalaenopsis, Oncidium,* and *Epidendrum;* among the terrestrials, *Paphiopedilum, Calanthe,* and some of the *Cymbidium* serve as examples.

Some terrestrial orchids growing in a European location.

Cultivation Needs

The previous chapter introduced us to how orchids live; now we will try to match our cultural practices to their lifestyles. The orchids that we will consider are only those that can be grown in the home or the greenhouse, basically the ones that grow in temperatures that rarely, if ever, reach below freezing. Orchids that come from colder climates, like the native lady's slipper, can be maintained only in the garden.

Light

The first and most important requirement for plant life is sunlight. Sunlight also provides heat, and, in fact, light and warmth are inseparable. Because we are growing our orchids in a synthetic climate, we have to handle these factors separately. Light (heat) is the principal requirement for growth, and growth depends on the assimilation of CO_2. Every plant grows within the confines of certain light (and temperature) requirements, and when light is insufficient, growth stops or the plant simply dies.

When we speak of light, we refer to particular wavelengths of electromagnetic rays. These rays transfer energy. When light touches an object, that energy is turned into one of its forms—heat, for example.

Different kinds of rays differ from each other in terms of wavelength—determined by the number of vibrations per second— also known as the light's frequency. The sensitive human eye limits what is visible in the light spectrum; further, this spectrum is divided into sections that the eye experiences as different colors. Short waves are violet, long are blue, with green, yellow, orange, and certain kinds of blue in between. Plants make the best use of light at the red and blue ends of the spectrum and lights designed for plant growth incorporate both ends. Light is absorbed, reflected, and filtered by plants, but only that light that is absorbed by the plants can be transformed into chemical energy.

To measure light, a special photocell is used that gives off current when struck by light rays; this current is measured. Light intensity is given in lumens or international candles: The number indicates the intensity with which a given surface is lighted.

There are practical, economic light meters on the market that are adequate for taking room light measurements.

2,000 to 3,000 lumens (or international footcandles) are the lower limit for normal growth. Outside, on a sunny summer day, the number of lumens is about 100,000. In the

Cultivation Needs

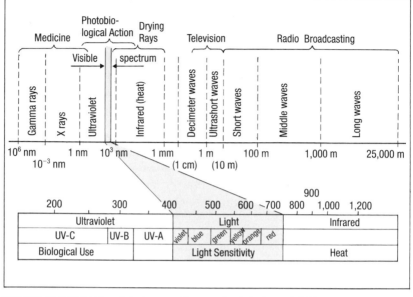

The photobiological action of electromagnetic rays extends far beyond visible radiant energy (light).

fall, the number drops to 30,000, and in winter to around 10,000. Unfortunately, there has been little systematic research done on the light requirements of orchids. Dividing them into plants that need a lot of light and plants needing less light is rather vague. In general, when we speak of orchids that require intense light, the requirement translates to between 20,000 and 45,000 lumens. Those that need less light require between 5,000 and 10,000. We know that it is

possible to grow orchids at 5,000 lumens—using only artificial light. Because the light in summer is much more intense, orchids grown in a bright window greenhouse or a greenhouse will need shading. In order to show how much light is available in a room, I took measurements on an August afternoon in the diffuse light of slightly overcast weather. Outside, the light measured 30,000 lumens, and under a tree it was only 3,000. In an unshaded greenhouse it was

23,000. The reading in the window facing west was 4,000; in the window facing south was 20,000; in the window facing east, 3,000; and in the window facing north, only 1,000. Available light in a window isn't always adequate, although sometimes people think that if anthuriens or African violets will bloom there, it will serve for orchids as well.

It is pretty easy to find out whether orchids will grow in a given situation, and by thinking back to your experience with other plants, which ones will grow well. If your African violet bloomed regularly, but your hibiscus sulked, then you know that only orchids with modest light requirements are possible; for example, *Paphiopedilum* and *Phalaenopsis*.

Besides light intensity, the duration of light is important. Plants in the tropics have twelve hours of light every day, all year long. In our climate in the winter months we have to augment natural light with artificial. We won't go into the various types of lamps available. As we

In this example, light intensity is reduced by three quarters each meter distant from its source. Here, light intensity at the window is 10,000 lumens; one meter away, the light measures only 2,500.

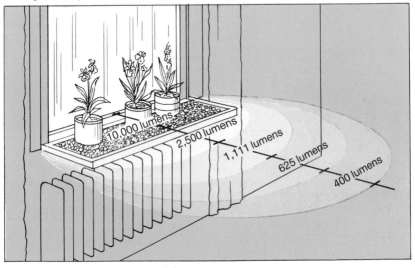

Cultivation Needs

have seen, plants use only certain segments of the spectrum. It is not only expensive, but less efficient to use regular incandescent bulbs instead of grow lights.

Depending on the use you intend for your grow lights—whether as supplementary light or as the main source—you can use the following points to help you decide which lamp to choose:

1. Purchase price.
2. Cost of maintenance.
3. Cost of electricity.
4. Purpose (greenhouse or room).

It is really only necessary to use supplementary artificial lights with a portion of your plants—those that are very young, those developing buds, those that are sick or freshly transplanted.

Temperature

Light and temperature are always correlated, and this fact is something to take into consideration when the heating is on. Plants can only use heat when adequate light is available to them. There is a minimum as well as a maximum temperature beyond which plant life fails. A temperature above 125° F (52° C) will destroy plants. In the course of evolution, orchids have adapted to fit into their native climates. Thus we make an effort to comply with the orchid's specific needs.

A plant accommodates the temperature of its environment through respiration. Generally, the plant's functions have a direct relationship to temperature. Orchids can come to harm when the temperature around them is significantly lower than their own. Even heat-loving orchids can be harmed in the open in summer.

Orchids come from every sort of climate. If we had to provide the optimum temperature for each, our collection would be severely limited. Fortunately, in practice, that isn't necessary, for orchids have demonstrated an amazing adaptability. Their temperature requirements can be divided into three classifications: cool, intermediate, and warm. Two exceptions are the *Cymbidium* and the so-called "cloud-forest orchids" (see page 107). The figures given in the following chart are only averages.

Naturally, higher or lower averages depend on the weather, and warm summer days can't be avoided.

Month	Cool	Intermediate	Warm
January	46–53	58–65	65–82
February	48–55	60–65	67–82
March	48–55	60–68	67–82
April	50–57	60–68	68–83
May	52–57	65–70	68–83
June	53–58	65–70	68–85
July	53–58	65–70	68–85
August	53–58	65–70	68–85
September	50–57	60–68	67–82
October	48–55	60–68	67–82
November	46–53	58–60	67–82
December	46–53	58–60	67–82

A temperature that drops about 5 or 6 degrees is especially important no matter to which temperature group the orchid may belong. Another reason for a drop in temperature is that it induces many orchids to set buds. Because we grow plants in containers, we have to consider that the temperature of the pot may in fact differ from the temperature of the air. Take care in window gardens that the dark pots that absorb the sun's rays don't heat up faster than the plants. The roots may be damaged. Keep the pots out of direct sunlight.

Air and Humidity

There is no other single factor in the culture of orchids that has led to greater error than the misunderstood concept of *humidity.* Humidity often is confused with moisture in the container. Copious water is given in an effort to emulate the high humidity of the tropics, and

Cultivation Needs

instead leads to the plants' demise.

First a little about air: An orchid, like all green plants, takes oxygen and carbon dioxide from the air. Both substances are absolutely essential to plant life. Photosynthesis changes light into chemical energy; hydrogen, oxygen, and carbon play decisive roles. How easy it is to forget that this procurement of energy and conversion of matter far exceeds the sum total of mankind's technically achieved energy. But what does this mean in terms of practical orchid care? Very simply, that it is up to you to make sure that there is enough fresh air and air movement.

There can be no growing room—whether greenhouse or window—without ventilation, and when orchid cases are used this is all too frequently forgotten. There has to be ventilation in winter, too—if it isn't too cold. Sometimes you'll have to heat and ventilate at the same time, regrettable but unavoidable.

Now we'll consider humidity. It is really better to say relative humidity, because without the "relative," the concept is incomplete. It defines the actual saturation of the air with moisture measured against a possible saturation.

Humidity is also inseparable from temperature, because the higher the temperature goes, the more moisture—water—that can be held in the air. An example: In 1 cubic meter of air, heated to 70°F (20°C), a maximum of 17.3 g of water can be held. In this case we could speak of a relative humidity of 100 percent. It follows that if the relative humidity is 50 percent, only 8.65 g of water have been taken into the air. In order to reach 100 percent relative humidity, an addition of 8.65 g of water are needed. The ability of air to retain water is, as we have mentioned, dependent upon temperature. At 42°F (5°C) the amount of water needed for complete saturation of a cubic meter is only 6.8 g. At 50°F (10°C) it has to be 9.4 g, and at 86°F the amount needed is 23.1 g. The cooler the air, the easier it is for the orchid grower to provide adequate humidity. Dry air encourages the plant to transpire heavily. To a certain degree transpiration is desirable because it gets water and food moving around in the body of the plant. When transpiration becomes too heavy, a smooth transport can no longer be achieved. The plant "droops," says the gardener.

How high should the humidity be for orchids? Total saturation is undesirable because it hinders transpiration. Unfortunately, there is no number that will work with every plant in every situation. Tempera-

Window trays improve humidity. This tray with a screen bottom ensures a secure footing.

ture plays a role. In a cool area, it isn't difficult to maintain a relative humidity of 80 percent, even in a room. On the contrary, we generally try to lower the humidity by ventilation and air movement. At 60°F (20°C) we are happy if we can achieve a relative humidity of 60 to 70 percent. These are averages, of course, and continual variations work actually to strengthen the orchid's defenses.

How can we achieve these conditions with our simple facilities? When we grow orchids in an open-window situation, a big help is the so-called plant or pebble tray. In the past, especially in the 50s, plant tubs, permanently installed and made of concrete or brick, were extremely popular. They were filled with peat, and houseplants (either with or without pots) were placed inside. At first the plants would thrive in such an atmosphere; lush growth, especially of the green plants, gave the impression of virgin forest. But very soon growth comes to a standstill, if the

Plants stand directly on the pebbles used to fill this tray. Pictured are some older but still beautiful varieties of *Paphiopedilum* species: *P.* 'Rossetii,' *P.* 'Maudiae,' and *P.* 'Leybournense.'

Cultivation Needs

plant doesn't die outright. The reasons for this sad situation lie in the souring and matting of the peat, and one of the most common errors in plant care: over-watering. Water can turn peat into a real swamp, and only complete replanting can save plants in this situation.

We can learn from errors like these. Plant tubs aren't bad by themselves, only the filling with peat and their use as growing containers are wrong.

It is difficult to install such a tub in a window and far easier simply to widen the windowsill and set out a flat tray of plastic or zinc-coated tin. This is a job that even a do-it-yourselfer with little experience can tackle. A radiator under the window no longer needs to create a dry-air problem, but instead it can be incorporated into a simple humidifying system.

Fill the tray with tuffa, gravel, or pebbles. (Small pieces of lava work well, too.) By filling the tray this way, the surface will be greatly increased, and it is this surface area that is responsible for the evaporation of water into the air. Keep the water level below the top surface of the pebbles.

The pots of orchids are set above the pebbles. It is best not to place them directly on the pebbles or they will wobble about, but on a screen of plastic or wood. The advantage of this method over the old tubs is enhanced evaporation (which provides humidity) and the ability to water each pot individually. Another advantage of this method is the plant communities that can be formed this way. The orchids themselves transpire and thus increase humidity, which is used by other plants in their community. If you have only one or two orchids, you may enlarge the plant community with other houseplants. Plants should never grow alone.

The radiator, acting as a kind of motor, provides bottom heat and stimulates evaporation. With a pebble tray, the area right around the plants will be 30 percent more humid than the rest of the room. The leaves of the plants act as a protective roof, limiting the area affected, and the orchid's air roots plump up in the high humidity. This method isn't only simple, it's also economical.

Fountains and room humidifiers are often offered to improve humidity—and they certainly do the job—but they are expensive, need to be maintained, and are only involved with the plants indirectly. A tray, on the other hand, makes watering and misting orchids even easier. The permanent planting tubs described earlier can also be put to good use, although they shouldn't be too deep, and if necessary a false bottom can be installed.

For those who find freestanding pots objectionable, there are jardinieres or planters. Just make sure that the plants get enough light. A simple wooden box, similar to the orchids' growing basket, is better.

Water

Water is the main component of all plants. Not only does it dissolve and carry chemical compounds, but it is also responsible for plant turgor and osmotic pressure. Of the water that a plant takes in, the largest portion is released through transpiration. If watering isn't undertaken, the plant wilts. While most important is the root absorption of water and the nutrients dissolved in it, even the green parts of a plant can absorb water. Damage to roots always has unpleasant results, and unfortunately, this kind of damage is caused by too much water. (See page 60.)

Water possesses different qualities. At one time rain water could be recommended for plants without any hesitation, but no longer, and today water needs to be tested for hardness, pH factor, and the presence of organic and inorganic substances. However, damage to orchids through bad-quality water happens less frequently than thought, and if you've never had a water problem with your houseplants, you'll have no trouble with orchids. It is those who have experimented too freely with growing orchids who have had poor results. Clean water free from organic materials can be had from ordinary drinking water. Chlorine can do some damage, but because it is a

Cultivation Needs

gas that has been added to water, it will diffuse if the water is left standing for 24 hours. At the same time, the water will warm up to the room temperature, necessary for watering.

Hard water is more of a problem. Magnesium and calcium compounds determine hardness, which is sometimes expressed in degrees. 10 mg of calcium carbonate per liter of water or 7.8 mg of magnesium carbonate create 1 degree of hardness. Soft water has 7 degrees of hardness, and hard water has nearly 21 degrees. For orchids the best kind of water is neither too hard nor too soft. Here, too, the planting medium can make a difference: Peaty soil tolerates hard water.

The hardness of water is not only a result of calcium and magnesium carbonate, but also of uncarbonated hardness, called permanent residual hardness. Sulfate and nitrate are contributing factors. Hardness due to carbons in the water can be boiled out; getting rid of other salts is more complicated. The pH value of water tells us how much hydrogen is available. Hardness plays a role here, too, because the more basic matter in the water, the higher the pH will rise above the neutral value of 7. Your local water works can give you information about the hardness and pH of your tap water. Most tropical fish stores carry preparations to make the necessary adjustments. Orchids prefer a slightly acid water with a pH of 5 to 6.

How do you lessen water hardness and change pH? With small quantities of water, the use of a packaged chemical preparation is the easiest. Running the water through a coffee machine first helps, but you'll still have to test for hardness and pH. For larger quantities of water, filtering a cubic meter of water through a ball of peat brings down the hardness considerably, and later this peat can be used in the garden. Another possibility is the addition of oxalic acid—but take care in using this. 22.5 g per cubic meter of water will reduce hardness somewhat (and reduce any calcium oxalate deficiency). Only those comfortable with chemicals should attempt working with concentrated hydrochloric acid (it's dangerous). 10 cubic centimeters of hydrochloric acid will bring down the hardness of 1 cubic meter of water. However, gypsum may form in the process. There is growing interest in salt removal through ion exchange (there is even a watering can equipped to do this). Salts are attracted to synthetic resin, which gives off other matter in exchange.

To include all methods, we mention both distillation and reverse osmosis, both expensive and only worthwhile for the grower with a very large collection.

The total amount of salts in water for orchids should never exceed 150 mg per liter. The signs of too much salt will be visible on damaged roots. The surface of the root will become brownish black, develop a crust, and appear to have been burnt, and the plant will harden and darken as well. If you suspect this situation, a soil-testing laboratory can run tests for you, and in addition have the water tested too. Your result will indicate the conductivity of water, something that can be ascertained by the instrument that measures it. The numerical value assigned to the water you had tested can be multiplied by 0.625 to obtain the salt content in ml per liter of water.

A special watering can with a filter battery.

Fertilizers

Like all other green plants, orchids take in fertilizer in both gas and liquid forms. The roots take in water, oxygen, minerals, and dissolved organic materials; the leaves take in carbon dioxide, hydrogen, and water containing fertilizer in solution.

Osmotic pressure in the root tissues enables the roots to make use of often very low concentrations of salts in the environment. Orchids have relatively limited powers of absorption, so that high salt concentrations around the root can have the reverse effect. Nutrients can be drained away from the plant—it will wilt and eventually die. Orchids number among the plants requiring great caution when fertilizing.

In addition to the passive, osmotic acquisition of nutrients, the active nutritive intake of mineral elements plays a large role. Ions in a watery solution are taken in. Using transpiratory energy (the active transport mechanism), the plant can absorb nutrients selectively. Why is this so important in orchid care? Because when we administer a fertilizer that contains all of the important nutrients, we put the ones it really needs at the orchid's disposal. The following is a list of the individual minerals, each listed briefly with a description of its effect on

Cultivation Needs

the plant. It is easy to find more information on this subject in horticultural literature.

Nitrogen

This is the important building block of egg white, chlorophyll, enzymes, and vitamins. Plants can synthesize organic nitrogen from inorganic sources. It is almost always in the form of nitrate or ammonia; other forms require prior preparation. Pure nitrate and ammonia guarantee a rapid uptake and rapid effects. The best time to fertilize is during a period of active growth. When nitrogen is deficient, older leaves turn yellow from the tip down, there is general chlorosis, and finally, the leaves die. Too much nitrogen is also dangerous. It produces a blue-green color, soft tissue, and an easily damaged orchid.

Phosphorus

This is an important component of simplified nucleic acid. It is responsible for the process of maturation of flowers and seeds, and for the formation of buds. Phosphorus is most often available in combination with potassium. It is virtually impossible to overfertilize. Use phosphorus toward the end of the period of active growth.

Potassium

Potassium is the most important ion in the maintenance of the plant's turgidity. A potassium deficiency shows up in the loss of turgor as transpiration and respiration increase. It is usually available in combination with other minerals.

Calcium

Calcium is another important plant-building material—especially for cell walls and root tissues. Lime binds potentially damaging salts in compounds that are hard to dissolve. Calcium is not considered particularly important in orchid culture. A deficiency may show up in connection with the use of peat and bark potting media.

Magnesium

Magnesium is found in cell fluids and in chlorophyll. Fertilize in combination with other minerals. (See above.)

Sulfur

This building material brings about general ionic activity in the plant and serves as a building block of many compounds. It is often found in combination with other minerals, such as nitrogen, phosphorus, and potassium. A deficiency is rare.

Iron

Generally iron is supplied in adequate quantities in the soil. In orchids its absence shows up in the chlorosis of young growth. It is important in manufacturing chlorophyll, in photosynthesis, and in transpiration.

The following minerals are usually abundant in normal fertilization; nevertheless, it doesn't do any harm to give a special dose of these trace elements: manganese, copper, zinc, molybdenum, chlorine, and boron.

Potting Material

We grow our houseplants in soil, a mixture of mineral and organic components. Of the latter the best thing is compost. These days, however, it is more often a standard potting mix with a peat base. Compost is the result of a natural decomposition process of organic elements (leaves, plant parts). Compost, like packaged soil, is used universally. If you are aware of a plant's particular needs in terms of soil composition, mixtures composed of all manner of ingredients may be produced. This is useful with orchids. The topic of soil composition is the most intensely discussed aspect of orchid care among growers—not only today, but even at the very beginnings of orchid culture. It is always surprising, but it happens over and over again—a new, euphorically praised potting medium or mix will be all the rage for a while and then quickly disappear.

It seems logical to supply orchids with soil from their native habitats, but you'll soon realize that this is impossible in practice—the multiplicity of orchids forbids it. Thus, every soil becomes a compromise between the absolute and the probable needs of a plant.

Cultivation Needs

Special orchid potting mixtures are commercially produced.

We know that most orchids grow as epiphytes—for them there is no soil. On their main stems, in the lower plant parts, and between the roots, humusy materials assemble and decompose rapidly, providing the orchid with nutrients. There is no comparison with the vast amounts of nourishment available in normal, humus-rich earth, but enough for these delicate orchids. Terrestrial orchids may also grow naturally in places with a thin layer of humus or an infertile substratum. An orchid under cultivation can have its needs more easily satisfied by the choice of an appropriate potting medium, and growers can usually acquire a ready-mixed medium designed especially for orchid cultivation. In addition, epiphytic orchids are also more easily grown in a container, if the medium approximates that of the plant's natural home.

We already know that air roots cannot live without oxygen; therefore, the foremost desired property of the potting mixture is a loose composition. Beyond that, the medium should possess structural stability, and it must be capable of holding water and nutrients. Naturally, it has to be free of any kind of harmful material, including chemicals and disease-carriers from the plant and animal kingdom. In order to meet all of these requirements, it may be necessary to mix together several materials.

The classic orchid potting medium, still useful today only difficult to obtain is osmunda fiber. It is composed of roots from the royal fern (*Osmunda regalis*) and the spotted fern (*Polypodium*). Both kinds are native to Europe. Tree ferns like Mexifern, Xaxin (*Dicksonia*), and Hapuu come from South and Central America. All have good structure, retain nutrients, and are slightly acidic (pH 5–6). *Sphagnum* is added, the wide-leafed species *S. squarrosum,* and *S. cuspidatum.* These mosses are quite acidic and capable of great water and air retention. As they disinte-

Cultivation Needs

Fern roots (Xaxim), an important part of all fern root-potting materials.

grate, they provide material for growth and have an antibacterial, antifungal action—they are useful homeopathically.

Partially decomposed beech leaves are added when epiphytes are grown, providing raw humus. With terrestrial orchids, small amounts of compost, loam, and sand can be added. Unfortunately, these supplements are both hard to find and expensive, and for commercial orchid nurseries they are out of the question. Generally, when you buy an orchid, the pot will contain some other substance—often a peat-based mix, commonly used in the garden industry. Other materials are added to a peat base as needed so that different mixtures can be assembled using one or more of the ingredients mentioned.

Peat
Advantages: It retains water and air, acts as a buffer, is free of seeds, and structurally stable. Disadvantages: It loses its oxygen retention when wet, is hard to wet when dry, but it can regain its ability to hold water if a little detergent is added to the water. Different types include peat fiber, fine peat, and shredded peat.

Black Peat
It is structurally stable, but should never be allowed to get completely dry. This can be a disadvantage in its resting period. Unfortunately, it doesn't hold water well and must always be mixed with fibrous materials, which cancels out its advantages.

Bark
All bark should be as free as possible from the heart material of the tree. Because of the rapid decomposition due to microorganisms, so much nitrogen and phosphorus is consumed, that a deficiency of these elements often arises. Bark

Cultivation Needs

is not only useful as supplemental potting material, but also when used alone. Good root growth more than compensates for the disadvantages of mineral deficiencies. Some of the available barks are:

- Conifer bark of European origin.
- Silva bark, also called orchid bark in the trade, cleaned and prepared from the bark of the North American Douglas fir.
- Vitabark, also American in origin, from *Abies concolor.*

Other fir tree barks include redfire bark, redwood, and others.

Meranti Planting Material
New kinds of growing media are being tried constantly, the latest being the shavings of a tropical wood for orchid potting material. It comes from an evergreen tree that can grow to a height of over 150 feet and attain a diameter of 6 feet, and it belongs to the genus *Shorea,* which includes several species from Southeast Asia. Trade names indicate origin (Lauan/Philippines, Meranti/Malaysia, and Seraya/Northern Borneo); all varieties mixed together are called Meranti (Red Meranti or Dark Red Meranti). The shavings are commonly used in window gardens. Exactly why they have achieved such enormous success

in the rooting of orchids is not clear. Mixes containing Meranti, or Meranti alone, can be used, and it is especially good for young plants and rooting. A nitrogen-heavy fertilizer is recommended.

Stones and Minerals
All of the materials listed below should be added for structural improvement.

- Pebbles and sand are useful for some terrestrial orchids to improve air circulation and structural stability.
- Hydroponic growing medium. It is important to heed instructions or possibly get information from the manufacturer. It ensures structural stability, allows for excellent air circulation, and retains water.
- Lava, generally offered as Eifellava. Its properties are similar to tuffa.
- Scoria, also of vulcanic origin. This medium is especially good for water and air circulation and is structurally stable. It binds nitrogen. Adequate fertilizer must be given; it is neutral to alkaline when combined with an acidic potting medium such as peat.
- Perlite, vulcanic, commercially prepared stone. These media are similar to scoria and are especially useful for young plants.

Some useful ingredients for orchid potting mixes: 1. Fine peat, 2. Bark, 3. Styropor, 4. Meranti, 5. Hydroponic medium.

Plastics

In the next few years, we can expect new products for orchid culture made from plastic. However, all attempts to grow orchids in plastic alone have sooner or later been abandoned, and providing complete nourishment with fertilizers available today is not possible for more than a year or two.

- Styropor (polystyrol foam), an important plastic material, useful for all types of potting mixes; it prevents compacting, is chemically neutral, and doesn't hold water—particularly important with peat mixes. It is also useful for a grower who habitually overwaters.

- Orchid Chips. Polystyrol, like styropor above, but with a rough surface to retain water. If used by itself, there is a constant need to fertilize.

The materials for orchid potting listed above are only a small portion of the best-known materials in use, and special mixes with regionally available materials are also employed. The decisive element is

Cultivation Needs

how these materials are put together, but on that subject opinions of orchid growers diverge widely. Water composition, place, price, and water retention play a big role. And, of course, it depends on which orchids will be grown in the particular material.

If the potting medium is supposed to serve as the source of nutrients, as is the case with the classic planting medium osmunda, then it can be assumed that only supplementary fertilization is needed. The pH value of the potting material determines which minerals are needed (again, the optimal pH level is 5–6). The desired results can be achieved by mixing the separate potting materials and the nutrients.

Containers

Now we will turn our attention to orchid containers. It wasn't very long ago that people thought that special orchid pots were needed in order to succeed in growing orchids, and of course plastic pots were unthinkable. Today, there is scarcely a single grower anywhere who still keeps plants in clay pots, with the exceptions of a few special botanical varieties. Whether price has anything to do with it, we'll soon see.

What did the classic orchid pot look like? It was baked clay, with several slits or holes on the sides, and a very large drainage hole. It also was the ideal solution for osmunda mixes. Soon standard clay pots crowded these special containers out. These were rather wide and flat (Azalea pots) and still an excellent container to use with osmunda fiber. But as the price of osmunda rose, peat was used more and more. Peat has to be fertilized, and here the clay pot began to pose problems: Water would evaporate through the porous clay, carrying with it dissolved fertilizer, and the concentrations of residual salts could quickly become dangerous for the orchids. They could be burned, and their roots could build up a salty crust that would eventually kill.

With a plastic pot, evaporation is

Cultivation Needs

Orchid containers, *from left:* osmunda pots, plastic pots, wooden baskets, clay pots.

only possible on the soil surface, where the salts are dissolved with every watering. Yet for some orchids (*Miltonia,* for example), even this small concentration can prove dangerous. Plastic is really the most practical with the newer potting materials, but you still must be careful not to select a pot that is too dark, that will warm too quickly in the sun. Usually brown or even gray to white pots can be found; unfortunately, many have thin walls of rather low quality, keeping them flexible for only a short time. Be-

cause orchids usually spend two years in a given pot, it's a good idea to buy the thickest, most flexible pot available—it saves trouble later on.

Wooden baskets are not only practical but decorative for orchid cultivation. An epiphytic orchid can find the most natural conditions for growth in a basket. Too, many varieties must have a basket because their blooms grow downward (*Stanhopea, Coryanthes*). However, only large chunks of potting material can be used in a basket

Cultivation Needs

without spilling out, and a basket requires frequent watering unless it is in a greenhouse. Water flows right through—sometimes enough to water the plants below. Further, the wood used in the basket may not be too soft; tropical woods such as pitch pine and teak are good.

Choose a basket large enough to hold your orchid for several years. Pseudobulbs whose roots grow over the edges will find nourishment easily enough in a basket. Chunks of potting material may be carefully added at any time. For a longer period of cultivation, fern root pots of xaxim are a good idea: They are both pot and soil. Fern fronds and stalks are also used. Epiphytic orchids can be tied in place; a nylon stocking cut into strips is excellent for this purpose. The strips need to be soft and to stretch, so the plant won't be damaged. It was once thought that planting material should be wedged in after the epiphyte was tied in place, but after much observation, the general opinion has shifted: The orchid is now set directly on its support. But a little sphagnum to encourage root growth will never hurt.

Of course orchids may be grown in other types of containers: Coconut shells, grape vines, the bark of the cork oak are only a few of many. There are no limits to the orchid grower's imagination, and it is basically both a matter of taste and pocketbook.

The popular epiphyte bark is really an artificial growing "container," too. Epiphytes grown on bark do well only when their immediate environment—a closed-window greenhouse, an orchid case, or a greenhouse—offers ideal growing conditions. Constantly spraying the plants has nothing to do with humidity.

When choosing a piece of bark on which to grow an epiphytic orchid, select one on which the plant can stay for many years. This means don't plant too close together and don't choose too small a piece.

In choosing such a piece of bark, you can use what is available locally. The best thing is an interesting, well-developed branch from a healthy, newly cut tree that hasn't yet begun to decompose. If the stem will be freestanding, it is going to need a good base. Holes can be bored into the lower part, and either rods or wire threaded through. Depending on the size of the trunk, a wooden box or plastic pot weighted with concrete can be installed beneath to make watering easier. Remember that later on, with all the orchids and their companion plants in place, the whole thing will be very heavy.

Clean the surface of the bark with a wire brush. Keep a sharp eye out

Orchids (*Phalaenopsis stuartiana*) are mounted on this trunk looking much as they would appear in the wild. *Behind* is the companion plant, Spanish moss, *Tillandsia usneoides*.

for pests. For the first two or three weeks, rinse the bark off frequently and thoroughly. Again, use nylon strips to tie on the plants. Bromeliads, ferns, or cacti (*Rhip-salis*) can be added.

A long-lasting epiphyte stand can be made from plastic pipe wrapped with the bark of Spanish cork oak. The plants are not tied on directly, but anchored in large or small hollows. This makes a good stand to use in an open garden window.

Growing Environments

In the previous chapters, special cultivation needs of orchids have been discussed, but putting these into practice is the grower's job. Some of these practices will be addressed again in the following chapter in relation to particular growing environments.

The Open-Window Garden

The best place in the home for houseplants and orchids is a window, and depending on the direction it faces, it can be optimal or just tolerable.

An open-window garden with intermediate-temperature orchids on a tray.

Practically speaking, the room where the window is located has much to do with which window to use; even a north window can be turned into a garden window with some technical help—you only have to know how. And a south window, ordinarily useful only for cacti and succulents, can be an ideal orchid window with a little shading. Basically, any window can be used, but it should be at least a square yard in size in order to admit adequate light. A wide windowsill serves best as a place to put containers, and for a do-it-yourselfer widening a sill shouldn't prove too difficult.

The window should also be ventilated. The ideal is ventilation without cold outside air coming into direct contact with the plants. Then, the window can be fitted with the kinds of growing trays described earlier. The very best space usage is when the tray has been custom-cut to suit the sill. The tray should be lined with zinc-coated tin. But take care, however, to avoid having the plants come into contact with tin; salts from the fertilizers can promote damaging combinations with the zinc.

The breadth of the tray depends on the size of the window. If the window size is about a square yard, the tray shouldn't be more than 12 inches wide; if it is 5 square yards, the tray can be 2 feet wide.

A closed-window greenhouse (the interior glass has been removed for the photograph): Orchids, bromeliads, and various green plants form a community.

If artificial lights are used, the depth of the area can be increased. The greater the light needs of the orchid, the closer it should be placed to the window, and those which need less light may be situated on the room side.

A really bright window always needs shading, and awnings or adjustable blinds work well. Additional light, especially in the dark winter months, improves growing conditions and provides the passerby with a planted stage setting in which orchids play the leading roles. With adequate available light, the top part of the window is where orchids and bromeliads may be hung. Spanish moss (*Tillandsia usneoides*) is a dramatic addition. Plant communities improve cultural conditions.

Growing Environments

The Closed-Window Greenhouse

By constructing one or several glass panels on the inside of the room, one can create an almost ideal climate for tropical orchids. (Remember when building this kind of arrangement to allow for easy access, or taking care of the plants will become an awful burden.) Setting up a window greenhouse is similar to that of the open-window garden. Supplementary light is useful. Because the window greenhouse temperature can diverge widely from that of the room, it's a good idea to include some type of heating—especially for warm-temperature orchids (see page 29); such heating should be independent of the room temperature. Too, the sun can quickly heat up a closed-window greenhouse, and then warm air has to be moved out. Openings for fresh air in the upper and in lower part of the window are needed, so an electric heater is probably the best solution overall. Other heating possibilities include cables, electrical radiators, and heating mats.

There is really no problem in providing the necessary relative humidity in a closed-window greenhouse. The air will saturate itself naturally from the cycle of watering and misting the orchids: Warm air rises and draws moisture from the pebble tray. It is necessary to provide for ventilation. In winter or at night, when the window isn't opened, a ventilator should provide air circulation to avoid possible fungal diseases.

Electric humidifiers can lighten the work and are especially recommended when the window greenhouse cannot be constantly heated. Fully automatic window greenhouses are not recommended because changes in temperature and humidity (naturally within a given range) promote good orchid health, raise immunity, and stimulate growth.

Orchid Cases

If turning a window into a growing area doesn't work, an orchid case may be the answer; it can only work, however, with adequate light. Most of the orchid cases offered commercially are unsuitable. For a group of plants with varying light needs there is usually only enough light to achieve miserable growth.

Orchids need light on a per-square-yard-of-surface basis—and depending upon the type of lamp, at least 400 to 500 watts. That means 6 to 8 fluorescent bulbs that are 1 yard in length and no further than 3 feet away from the plants. Problems arise from their housing. Ceiling screens or plates of milk glass that hide the bulbs also cut down on the light. And the size of the plants that can be grown in an orchid case greatly limits the selection. A case you build yourself may not be as decorative, but will serve cultivation

An attractively appointed orchid case.

Growing Environments

needs better. It can be custom-designed to include green plants, a tree trunk for epiphytes, and whatever else is desired.

As with the window greenhouse, you'll have to consider heating that can be regulated, and most important, ventilation. Again, humidity is not a problem, and a ventilator to circulate air isn't absolutely necessary.

An orchid case as an auxiliary space along with open-window cultivation is an excellent solution. It can display the jewels of the collection—the blooming plants. Later on, they can be returned to the window. The orchid case provides a truly tropical environment that is easily visible and for the duration of the bloom is the optimal setting.

Growing Under Lights

Growing under lights can augment other growth areas. It is also possible to do so in an area with no other available light. Experienced orchid growers have used lights for every part of the orchid's development—from seedling to a mature plant. In order to provide enough light, special grow lights are commercially available. In this situation, it isn't the way it looks but how well it works that is the main consideration. High electricity bills even out because heating costs are lowered if outside surfaces do lose warmth. Generally speaking, growing under lights is best employed as a supplement to other methods. Have an expert give you advice on lighting and watering.

If you've ever dreamed of an indoor swimming pool, surrounded by palms and orchids—forget it. It is only a beautiful dream. Not only is it too expensive, but orchids won't grow around the average swimming pool. The even temperature, the constantly high humidity, not to mention the chlorine fumes and the lack of light, make it impossible to grow orchids around that dream pool; dream about houseplants instead.

Growing Environments

Conservatories and Sun Rooms

There's nothing new under the sun, and in the case of the sun room that developed from the conservatory the statement is true. The roots of the conservatory go back to the beginning of the nineteenth century. It is also true that the sun room is the environment in which orchids have the brightest future. "Build with the sun," "solar greenhouses save energy"—these are the kinds of things we read about in building magazines. The transformation of the lean-to greenhouse is hardly recognizable. Anyway, how did the sun room evolve? At the end of the nineteenth century, it was all the rage to be surrounded with exotic plants. Often it was less for a love of plants than for fashion and status. Care of these exotic and expensive items wasn't possible in the dark interior of the home, and a greenhouse was affordable to only the wealthy because heating and care were outrageously costly in that era. Nevertheless, one had to have plants to loll about under the palms. A small balcony or veranda was glassed in and the conservatory was begun, a kind of forest under glass. The development of increasingly large and then room-sized conservatories began as plant rooms that ended as sun rooms.

Greenhouse used as a sun room.

When these rooms first began to the used all year long, cold-tolerant plants like palms were grown. What should we think about when siting a sun room? First, it should be on the brightest side of the house. The location of the garden is important; free access to the garden is desirable and makes plant care easier. Of course, it is also possible to have a raised sun room on a roof or balcony. Check with local zoning regulations first. The material that allows light into the room should be as expansive as possible. Whether glass or plastic roof and walls are used is a financial question. Double panes insulate best and are recommended; for safety's sake, wire glass is a possibility that provides shade as well.

Growing Environments

The roof should be pitched to eliminate dripping condensation, which will make staying and caring for plants in the sun room unpleasant. Shading must be used. Outside shade is best and keeps the room from overheating. Ventilation is rarely a problem. The floor should be composed of a waterproof material. The best materials are dark tiles that hold warmth and are nonreflective. Rattan or bamboo furniture—and also wooden or plastic—should suit the damp plant environment. Heating that suits the ideal temperature of the orchids should be installed, the easiest being an extension of the house's heating system.

Decorating with epiphyte trunks, fountains, planting beds, and tables is a matter of taste. In any case, the plant room will soon be the center of the home. Cool-climate orchids especially can have their cultivation needs met in this setting.

As opposed to maintaining a greenhouse, costs of a sun room are still affordable. The lines between conservatory, lean-to greenhouse, or sun room aren't always clear: The more the room is used for plant care, the more likely we are to call it a greenhouse or conservatory than to call it a sun room.

The Freestanding Greenhouse

Growing orchids in a freestanding greenhouse is the optimal cultivation environment. Sooner or later every orchid grower develops the wish for a greenhouse, and often it is realized as a means of containing a plant collection that has grown unworkable elsewhere.

The high costs of installation and maintenance scare many orchid growers away. But many hobbies are expensive, whether racing cars or world travel. Concerning the various energy costs (which depend on climate and type of heating), I would like to include some personal experience. Our greenhouse is slightly under 900 square feet and is used half the time as a warm house, the other half as a cool house. The costs of heating both types of houses are high, but always the same. This isn't an absolute rule, but will give you some idea of relative costs.

The development of the freestanding greenhouse in the past ten years has been revolutionary. Once the manufacturers were almost exclusively English, and the house models all English. Now there is a well-developed market here, with products suitable for the wide range of American climates.

An orchid greenhouse really isn't a different type of house, but it

A *Phalaenopsis* collection is housed in the warm section of a small greenhouse. A table with raised shelves makes care and display easier.

should have certain features. The folk advice "cheap can get expensive" is to be taken to heart when purchasing a greenhouse: It is more often the maintenance costs than the purchase price that discourages the use of greenhouses. A greenhouse should be the orchid grower's source of pleasure, not stress. Although we can only touch upon a few types of greenhouses here, there are many available, and you should certainly go comparison shopping. Try to find out from the manufacturer if there is someone in your neighborhood who has had experience with the product. Especially in terms of heating costs, another's experiences can be extremely valuable.

Investigate the modular greenhouses that allow for enlargement later on. The price will largely depend on the type of construction—whether wood, steel, plastic, or aluminum. In winter, the orchids need much light, and that is when the widths of the supports makes a difference. Too, steel and aluminum transfer cold and can negate the effect of the heat-retaining roof.

All parts that come into contact with the outside air have to be insulated. That doors and ventilating windows should close tightly goes without saying, but in practice it is rarely the case. The roof should be consistent with the rest of the construction. Houses made for single panes of glass cannot simply be fitted with double glass later, and while double panes made of plastic have good insulating qualities, they do not have a very long life. Make

Growing Environments

sure that you get a guarantee for the life of the house.

Good ventilation is an important cultivation need; whether under a roof or built into the roof itself depends on the temperature at which you will keep your house. Cool houses almost always use under-roof or side windows. Tables in the greenhouse made with wooden slats or wire screening are the best. These shouldn't be wider than 32 inches or individual plants will be awkward to reach.

The siting of the greenhouse is an important consideration. Traditionally, a north-to-south orientation is avoided to maximize the amount of light in winter, and in summer the greenhouse must be shaded anyway. More important is the free position—not in the shade of the home or trees.

Accessibility and proximity of heating are also important. Keep a path at least two feet wide so that daily chores don't become the running of an obstacle course. Make sure that your heating system allows for lowering the temperature at night. Let an expert handle the installation of electrical appliances, and let the manufacturer adjust the heating. Only firms that have done extensive greenhouse construction have the experience needed to handle a heating system so different from the ordinary house type. Air circulated by a ventilator

through closable flaps is especially useful in a well-insulated greenhouse. Humidifiers are superfluous, useful only to lighten the chores when the caretaker is away. Self-watering and drip irrigation systems are not for the orchid hobbyist.

Recently, there has been much talk about solar greenhouses. What the talk is about is greenhouses (generally the lean-to variety) in which energy is stored and utilized for heating purposes. The solar approach is better suited to vegetables than orchids, but you should nevertheless follow their development; the solar greenhouse is a promising concept that just isn't practical as yet for orchids.

Growing Environments

Vanda Rothschildiana, a cross of *V. coerulea* × *V. sanderiana* (1931), one of the parents of the "blue" *Vanda* hybrids.

Caring for Orchids

You'll often hear about someone who diligently follows all the rules, but can't keep his plants alive. And we all know someone else with such a green thumb that everything he looks at blooms. All manner of recipes for success—from secret fertilizers to the right music—are passed about. At the very least, so it's claimed, you have to talk to your plants.

Among orchid lovers it's the same: Whenever two meet, secret tips are exchanged. These may concern technical aspects of orchid care, such as the preparation of water or supplemental lighting, or the addition of certain mineral-

An *Oncidium* hybrid blooms in the author's greenhouse. The ventilator in the background eliminates stagnant air—important for healthy plants.

Caring for Orchids

containing supplements such as eggshell to the fertilizer. Unfortunately, the hoped-for effect doesn't always follow—it just doesn't work. And now you'd like to hear the real answer, in that we are so used to having our problems solved with good solid information about what to do in any given situation. Science has investigated all aspects of plant life. Okay—how about some clear-cut instructions for orchids? As luck would have it, orchids don't lend themselves to easy answers. The best we can do is give you guidance in caring for them. The most important advice is *patience.* Orchids grow slowly, and respond just as slowly to our care; they also die slowly. If you do something wrong, it won't be immediately noticeable. Patience means watching the orchids, learning to anticipate their needs, and this is the only kind of advice that this book can give you.

Orchids thrive in every kind of climate, but in the long run a combination of orchids with similar needs offers the best chance of success. However, limiting your collection to a single type doesn't mean it will be a lackluster group of similar plants from the same genus, all of which bloom at the same time. Absolutely not. Whether you choose the cool, intermediate, or warm groups, the selection is so immense that no collection could unify them. And every home has a different set of conditions that suit different groups of individuals. Compare the temperature in your growing area with the list on page 29. Then you can judge which group of plants is right for your home conditions. The descriptions of the main genera will make it possible for you to assemble a group of plants with similar cultivation needs. This grouping by need is important not only in home plant cultivation, but also in sun room or greenhouse settings as well.

It would seem that the easiest approach would be growing a single genus, but with orchids it isn't that simple. The genus *Oncidium* has species that grow in cool, intermediate, and warm climates—not to mention the *Oncidium* hybrids. There is no answer to the question "How do I grow orchids?" because there is no typical orchid: We always deal in specifics.

When you buy a plant it is very important to learn its correct name and how to care for it. By crossing many genera, a universal kind of orchid actually is emerging, one that adapts well to different conditions. Frequently genera and species from diverse climates are crossed, and the only clue to their care is careful observation. The grower will learn soon enough whether the orchid is doing well. All young plants, older

Caring for Orchids

pseudobulbs, and recently transplanted orchids enjoy a somewhat warmer situation. And here is another important point: Orchids aren't loners, they grow best in a community. And they're not fussy about their neighbors, whether rubber tree, fern, or begonia—all are welcome. Naturally, companion plants should share the same temperature needs. Above all, the bromeliads make decorative and natural companion plants for tropical orchids.

Are There Easy Orchids?

Your first experience with orchids should be with an "easy orchid." Many orchid nurseries advertise them, but in reality such an orchid doesn't exist: "Easy" is what a given orchid grower has found easy to grow in a given setting. Like the "typical" orchid, there is no single orchid that will be "easy" for all.

When buying an orchid, indicate which temperature you can provide (cool, intermediate, or warm), then let the nursery offer you a selection. Your first orchid should be a strong bloomer. Make absolutely sure of its Latin name, so that you can obtain correct information about its care. If you are offered a budded plant, make sure that it is immature enough to toler-

ate a move. Ask about its particular light requirements and get its cultivation information in writing. Learn the length of its blooming time to avoid disappointment later. And above all, if it doesn't work the first time, don't forget that orchids demand patience.

The Resting Stage

When you read about orchids, you'll frequently come across the advice that orchids have defined rest periods, sometimes a period several months long. What is meant is that orchids living in the wild often go through a period in which the natural climate conditions do not foster active growth. We see this same thing happen in our gardens with perennial plants, when some of them lose their leaves with the first frost. Among the tropical orchids, too, there are some that will drop leaves during the resting period, although pseudobulbs remain.

It does seem difficult to determine when the resting period ends. Because of the artificial climate conditions in a home or greenhouse, the plant's rhythm may become confused, and the orchid just keeps going. Ascertaining the resting period is even trickier with crosses from several genera, which often develop an atypical

Right, a young, new shoot.

and fully new rhythm. This new rhythm may be totally independent of our climate with its high light intensity in summer and low light intensity in winter. A rest period is necessary for almost all bulbous orchids because that is when flower buds develop. Sometimes resting just means a 3- to 5-degree drop in temperature, as with *Phalaenopsis*. Others, such as those from the Himalayas, go through a resting period with the temperature lowered by 50 degrees or more.

Let's simply observe the orchid's growth cycle. With increasing light or warmth from our heating system, root growth begins: We notice new root tips at the neck of the pseudobulb or on the shoots of monopodial plants. What follows is the leafing out—a new leaf develops (in *Phalaenopsis* this is called the bud leaf). This is the end of the resting phase; now we give the plant all that it needs for optimal growth (water, light, heat, and nutrients).

Growth is almost complete; a bud has developed. The orchid will soon begin its resting phase.

Caring for Orchids

The fresh, light green of new growth is easy to recognize. Some orchids develop blooms at the same time *(Zygopetalum, Lycaste).* Over the next few weeks, growth continues, leaves develop, and the pseudobulb forms. Eventually, the fresh green turns darker and begins to resemble the older leaves. At the end of its growth period newer shoots will be as large or larger than the old ones. The dark color of the leaves is conspicuous. No matter what the time of year outside, the resting period is due to begin. This means we'll have to cut down on watering, reduce the fertilizing, and lower the temperature according to the needs of the particular plant. The monopodial species, too, will pass through similar phases—only the mature leaves are the signal. The rest period ends when growth begins again. It doesn't matter how long it lasted; we are only observers and must wait for the orchids to make the first moves. Almost all orchids have a resting period, and the length of time depends on the individual plant.

Again, here is where the most errors are made.

Watering

How often should one water? This is the most commonly asked question. Incorrect watering is the main cause of trouble with houseplants, and orchids are no exception. Water quality is less important than the frequency of watering. Again, there is no single answer to the question—no simple solution. How much and how frequently you should water depends on the following:

- Potting medium (see page 37): The main ingredient is the decisive one; peat holds moisture longer than osmunda fiber. And the condition of the medium makes a difference, too; freshly planted orchids dry out more quickly than those growing in an older medium.
- Container: A plastic pot holds moisture longer than a clay pot, and much longer than a wooden basket. Size of the container makes a difference, too.
- Room temperature: In a warmer room, an orchid transpires more than in a cool room.
- Season: Here we refer to the season of growth. Many orchids grow actively over the winter, needing more water at that time.
- Size: Small plants require less water than larger ones, because their respiratory surface is smaller.

Caring for Orchids

A watering can with an especially long spout is absolutely necessary in a greenhouse.

The daily decision whether to water or not is the most important job of the grower. There are measuring devices, but these are of no use for orchids. Not only could these devices damage roots and carry disease, they just won't work in an orchid medium. They only probe the degree of moisture they contact. Since orchid plant media are generally porous, their surfaces dry out relatively quickly even though the inside of the pot may remain moist. The permeability of the medium is deceptive—it looks like all the water simply runs right through the container. But that is only the way it looks.

When testing whether to water, the green thumb or finger is an important tool. Try to insert it as deeply into the medium as possible without damaging roots. There, the warm finger can feel the cool moisture of the medium. If moisture is clearly discernible, no watering is needed—even if the upper surface is completely dry!

Naturally, this kind of test is impractical with a very large collection, but with a little more experience it may not be needed. The condition of the medium, the phase of growth, and the season determine *if* and *how much* should be watered.

Because they are uncertain how and when to water, many orchid growers just spray their plants frequently but lightly in the hope of not doing anything wrong. In theory, spraying should work, but often it leads instead to a cycle of constant spraying that, in turn, could result in eventual saturation. It is true that orchids take in water through their leaves, but only a little; the main water intake is through the roots. As has already been stated, most orchids are overwatered. Indeed, it is difficult to control the grower's urge always to be doing something. He thinks, *A little more won't hurt—tomorrow*

Caring for Orchids

I won't water as much. Basically, the plant cannot stockpile water. All that that extra water does is flow through the medium, wetting it, and removing oxygen from the container. Roots can't breathe and die. The plant then begins to wilt—always a sign of root damage, even when it has other causes. Often, the wilted appearance leads to even more watering and then the orchid's demise.

A simple and practical method to counteract overwatering is the addition of styropor to the potting medium. No matter which other ingredients are used, styropor can be mixed in to a 50 percent concentration. This type of medium is almost foolproof and can be especially useful for beginners. Badly overwatered plants benefit from a speedy transplant into new, dry potting medium.

Fertilizing

It wasn't so very long ago that people thought orchids didn't need fertilizing. Now we know that orchids are light feeders that were adequately nourished when the classic potting media were used. Through decomposition, nutrients were constantly available. Supplemental fertilizing with very small amounts of organic products was also done.

Today, because the modern potting media only provide inconsequential nutrients, fertilizing is absolutely necessary. It is very easy to fertilize using the premeasured packaged types available for orchids: Gabi, BEGA, Orchid-quick. Pretty soon, however, the orchid grower may find that though he provides the optimal fertilizer, the optimal results are no longer possible. This is because of the potting medium, the conditions of growth, and, not least, water quality. A blend of fertilizers as well as a mixture of potting media may help.

We never use orchid fertilizer full strength. If the manufacturer of a special orchid fertilizer suggests 2 teaspoons of fertilizer per liter, add only 1. With all media, except osmunda, fertilize each third time you water.

The proportions of the basic minerals (nitrogen : phosphorus : potassium) are 2 : 1 : 1 for orchids;

Caring for Orchids

Organic plant care items and fertilizers are easy on plants.

this combination is fine for a well-rooted orchid in active growth. For young plants, increase the nitrogen to a 3:1:1 combination, and with Meranti and bark media use 4–6:1:1. Peat media will need lime. When the shoots are fully developed (generally late summer), the proportion of nitrogen should be reduced.

Adding lime is especially important with peat and bark media; when these two are mixed, 3 to 5 g of lime should be added to each liter of mix. Add liquid lime every six months or so (2 g lime per liter water). Another possibility is the direct strewing of lime on the pot (1 teaspoon every six months for a 4-inch pot). Many orchids (*Paphiopedilum niveum* and some close relatives) occur naturally in a limey soil. Generally, orchids do not dislike lime.

Leaves are also capable of absorbing fertilizer. This is a good thing to remember when fertilizing plants that have been newly transplanted. 0.5 g of a complete fertilizer is dissolved in 1 liter of water. The plant can then be sprayed with this solution. Don't fertilize if the plant looks sick (look for reasons why), is in full sun, or if the pH is too low (lime first).

Caring for Orchids

Now, a bit of my own personal experience with organic fertilizers. Orchids are a hobby that will occupy many years. Quick results, the kind to be had with a shot of a particular mineral, should never take the place of a careful and regular supply of all the necessary nutrients placed at the plant's disposal. This way your orchids will give you years, even decades, of pleasure.

It is no secret that many natural orchid types (*Encyclia vitellinum, Cattleya citrina, Oncidium varicosum*) can only be kept alive by using organic fertilizer. By-products of the natural decomposition of organic fertilizers are substances that haven't been investigated thoroughly enough. Whether guano or cottonseed meal (to name just two), all have a harmonious relationship of the basic nutrients in addition to all of the trace elements. This type of fertilizer works slowly and lasts a long time, working better in the long run. Whether beginner or experienced grower, the organic fertilizers work best for orchids. Too much experimenting with fertilizer has cost the lives of many plants.

Light and Shade

In an effort to provide and maintain the proper humidity for the plants, the beginning orchid grower has a tendency to cut them off from fresh air altogether. This tendency is heightened during the cold days and nights of winter. But fresh air is necessary for successful growth. Whether plants are situated in a window or in a greenhouse, plants should be aired whenever the outside temperature permits. You have to watch, of course, that the cold winter air doesn't blow directly on the plants, and frost is a real danger that can quickly damage plants. The ideal situation is one that allows the plants air from on overhead ventilator, or a side window that swings out can serve this purpose well.

A little advice for greenhouse owners: Diffused light and direct sunlight can heat up a greenhouse to 95° or more. Because the plants appear to be in danger, the first response is often to open all the windows and doors to lower the temperature. Wrong. It is true that the temperature will be lowered a few degrees if everything is opened up; but the humidity will bottom out. The plants will respond by transpiring heavily, giving out more moisture than their roots can take in. Therefore, it is important not to open all the windows

A nonelectric, automatic ventilator for use in the greenhouse.

and especially not the door. Instead, heighten the humidity to avoid wilting. Most of the time a simple wetting down of the paths, tables, and floor works well. A sprayer fitted above the floor can be very helpful.

As we already know, most orchids grow in semishade. Plants, particularly those which come into direct sunlight after months of poor winter light, can quickly burn. If you see a reddish coloration on the leaves, you know there is too much light. Sometimes panes of today's insulated glass work like a magnifying glass. There should be a shade for every window. A jalousie or blind works well, especially if it is adjustable; sometimes a simple sheer curtain will do the job.

A greenhouse or sun room needs shade through the summer months. If the shades are adjustable, it will be useful on overcast days. Basically, shading the glass from the outside is always the best solution. The sun's rays are reflected off the greenhouse and the heat is reduced. Inside shades hamper ventilation on many greenhouses, making inside treatments second best, and temporary shading by painting on whitewash is not enough for orchids. Shading fabric made of rot-proof, UV-resistant polyethylene has proven itself and it comes in different grades of light permeability. Light-hungry orchids would need a 50 percent reduction; others, 75 percent.

Caring for Orchids

Transplanting

Like all other houseplants that only have the restricted area of their container at their disposal, orchids must be transplanted from time to time. But transplanting is something done only when it can no longer be avoided. With orchids this is usually every two years, depending upon the genus. Except in the event of a plant's being too wet, an orchid needs transplanting when:

- The pot has no more room for the forthcoming growth period.
- New growth has already grown over the side of the pot (see photo 1).

1

- The potting medium is compacted, whether from natural decomposition, an incorrect mixture, or from errors in watering or fertilizing. The grower may recognize compaction by the appearance of the top surface as well as a constantly wet substratum.
- Quick growth is desired, regardless of flower development.

Choosing the right moment to transplant is important, a time determined by the orchid itself, rather than by the season. As we already know, orchids form roots only once during their growth period, and the first sign of this new growth is also the signal to transplant. New shoots develop when the roots do, which can be seen when the shoots in orchids that form pseudobulbs swell and new leaves (bud leaves) in the monopodials appear. If transplanting is not done at precisely the right moment, orchids such as *Paphiopedilum* won't develop any roots at all. If the roots are no more than ¼ to ⅔ of an inch long, there is only the slightest danger of damaging them during transplanting and we can take up the work.

Caring for Orchids

Prepare the new potting medium and a new, clean container in preparation for transplanting. They should be sterilized. One day before transplanting, wet the medium so that it can be compressed like a snowball, but still stays loose and (especially packaged mixes) can be mixed easily. The plant to be repotted should also be prepared. On the preceeding day, water it thoroughly and fertilize (only healthy plants).

Before you begin the actual work, prepare any necessary dips; these serve to eliminate pests where necessary. Take care when using these substances! Always wear rubber gloves, and whatever you use a dip consult the section "Pests and Diseases" first (see page 71). In any case, roots and cut places must be treated with a fungicide, and charcoal is useful in this regard.

Carefully remove the orchid from its container. It may be necessary to break a clay pot (see photo 2). Most often, the plant will slip easily from its pot (photo 3). Then remove as much of the old medium as possible. Be careful: The roots should not be damaged. Don't rip

2

3

4

5

Caring for Orchids

bits of remaining medium from the roots. Use a sharp rose clippers— no squeezing, just a good, clean cut—on all rotten roots and plant parts. Cut back into healthy tissue. If necessary and possible, divide the orchid (photos 4 and 5; see also page 77).

Now choose the right sized pot. Sympodially growing plants need enough room for two new pseudobulbs; repot monopodials in pots that are two sizes, or one inch, larger. Measure—don't guess—or the one you choose will almost always be too large. Later it will be too hard to water. Use the rose clippers to trim all roots that don't fit into the new container and that would otherwise break (photos 6 and 7).

Now lay the plant in the dip so that all of the cut places are covered. Then place the orchid on some newspaper to dry, possibly covering it against sun and drafts. When it is dry, you can continue the procedure. Put a couple of inches of styropor into the pot for drainage (photo 8). Orchids with long pseudobulbs (*Dendrobium, Chysis*) need heavier pebbles for drainage; these also serve as ballast to keep the pot from tipping over.

If the orchids have barely any roots, they should be bound to a stake and set in the container. A "root" can also be built of wire: It should be stretched around the plant in a "u" form, so that both ends help to hold the plant in place.

Now the plant is placed in the pot. Sympodial orchids (photo 9) are set so that the oldest pseudobulb touches the side of the pot in order to give room for the new ones to develop. Monopodial orchids, like *Phalaenopsis,* are situated in the middle of the pot.

The new medium should be placed between the roots with great caution (photo 10); press down as you go so that later the roots won't be snapped off. Depending on the medium, the coarsest material should go directly above the drainage layer; most of the time it will be on the outside of the pile of medium. Then add the finer components. When using fibrous medium (osmunda), a wooden stick is helpful to push bits of fiber between the roots. Peat, bark, and meranti can be simply shaken and pseudobulbs (*Dendrobium, Chysis*) need heavier pebbles for drainage; these also serve as ballast to keep the pot from tipping over.

Avoid burying the plant alive, but great gaping holes are also undesirable. Tap the pot to shake loose medium down into any holes. Unlike the customary procedure with houseplants, orchids are not watered at this time; the medium should still be moist enough. Dryer conditions encourage the formation of scar tissue on the severed roots and pseudobulbs. In the next 3 to 4 days, mist or spray only. You may include a fertilizer in the spray solution. Keep the humidity high and provide shade and warmth; a plastic bag can be put over a single pot to limit transpiration—and give it a bit of air, too.

Whether or not you should divide an orchid when repotting depends on the following: If it isn't divided, will the plant grow too large for its space? Do you want more plants? Are the old pseudobulbs or leaves in bad condition? Only undertake a division for these reasons. Larger plants bloom much better. Excep-

Caring for Orchids

tions to these rules can be found on page 78.

When dividing, leave no more than three leafless pseudobulbs on each piece. Cutting off an old pseudobulb (rejuvenation) is only done when there are many more leafless pseudobulbs than those with leaves.

Vacation Care

Many people won't grow orchids because they cannot care for them during an absence. There isn't always a friendly neighbor around, and sometimes even when there is, the plants suffer from too much care. Orchids are pretty sturdy and can easily go for a week if shading and heating has been provided. If the absence is going to be longer, there is a simple solution: Group plants around a pail of water. Wool yarn, one or more strands depending upon water needs, are strung from the pail of water to the orchid pots. One end is pushed deeply into the medium with a needle (with houseplants, it is usually laid on the surface). Orchid media won't transfer moisture as readily as the usual potting soils.

If you have a greenhouse, there is no getting around asking a friend or neighbor for help. Give your friend good instructions. Make sure he or she knows how to water.

You can use a color code to indicate which plants need what care. Red might indicate they are to be watered once per week, green, twice weekly, and so on. Remember that too little water is less damaging than too much. If the weather remains overcast they can go even longer without being watered.

In the winter plants with pseudobulbs can go for several weeks without water. At this time, all your plant-sitter will have to do is maintain the heat and make sure there is enough humidity and light.

Pests and Diseases

It is not the purpose of this book to cover all the possible diseases of orchids, and the diagnosis of disease should usually be done by an expert. It should be stressed that the orchid's susceptibility to disease is not nearly as great as that of the typical houseplant.

What is important with orchids is prevention through the maintenance of the appropriate cultivation needs. When sickness does appear in an orchid, it is usually traced to incorrect cultivation practices rather than to genuine pests. Naturally, a plant in a weakened condition is more likely to fall prey to pests.

As with other plants, orchid problems can be divided into three sources: plants, animals, and viruses.

Virus Diseases

Viruses—Here is a word to strike terror into the orchid lover's heart. Viruses are responsible for different diseases in orchids. Some of the more common ones are *Cymbidium* mosaic virus, *Odontoglossum* ringspot virus, or tobacco mosaic virus, to name only a few. A horticulturist is the person to diagnose these diseases. A quick and exact diagnosis is possible using an electron microscope. Is it a virus? The outer symptoms

These three photos show orchid blossoms that are deformed, a sign of virus disease.
Above: Malformation of the petals of *Phalaenopsis.*

Center: A *Doritaenopsis* with a double lip.

Below: Malformation of the petals of *Cattleya.*

Caring for Orchids

cannot constitute the final diagnosis. In the three examples of malformed orchids that indicate virus disease, only one was really infected (*Cattleya* with *Cymbidium* mosaic). The grower's job lies in prevention of disease through plant hygiene. Use only sterile tools when cutting plants; they can be put through a flame or heated in the oven to 250°C. Another useful tool is the Japanese knife, a razor with a metal handle.

Viruses are transferred through the plant's sap. To date, there is no chemical means of fighting viruses; insects, aphids, snails, and the like are virus carriers, and fighting them is of necessity. If your plant is the victim of a virus, the only solution is complete destruction of the plant by burning.

Bacteria and Fungi as Causes of Disease

Of the diseases introduced to plants by plants, bacteria are the causes of many. They are difficult to trace, and, unfortunately, often discovered too late. They can be spread by water, wind, plants, or potting media that are already infected. They are almost always to be found on healthy plants, but swarm into the plant tissue when damage has occurred (errors in care, wounds).

Typical symptoms are slimy, wet places on leaves and pseudobulbs. The tissues become yellow and translucent until finally the whole plant dies. Rather than worrying about whether the plant is suffering from *Pseudomonas, Erwinia,* or another bacteria, grab the spray bottle of Orthocide-50 or -84 and follow the manufacturer's instructions. Preventive measures are air circulation, fresh air, careful watering, and even temperature. In addition to bacteria, fungal diseases pose a problem, and more than a hundred such diseases have been described. Because fungi

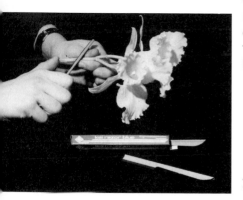

A disposable Japanese knife doesn't carry viruses because it is used only once.

and bacteria often occur simultaneously, the diagnosis is extremely difficult to make and impossible for the layman. High humidity (important for orchids) also fosters fungal life.

Damping off and black rot affect mainly young plants. Blight is found in many plants, among them *Phalaenopsis,* especially when transplanting. The leaves exhibit watery gray flecks; next, a portion of the tissue is attacked, and very soon fungi have covered the entire plant. Root rot as a result of incorrect watering is also not uncommon. Once more, the actual damage is done by a fungus or a bacterium, but there is always some oversight in the care that paves the way for disease. Sometimes flower speck is found on a blossom—often an attack of *Botrytis* or *Fusarium* or both. Small brown or brownish black points appear. It is especially prevalent in the transition period before the heat is turned on. Lowering the humidity and increasing air circulation are the best things to do.

Proven remedies include Benomyl, Captal (Orthocide-50/-84), and Polyram-combi. Always follow the manufacturer's directions; these remedies are poisonous.

Insect Damage

To an inexperienced grower, an insect attack comes on like a bolt out of the blue—especially because insects move quickly. Aphids are easy to see. Red spiders are more difficult and they are very frequently found around orchids. Their fine webs and the places where they feed are recognizable as a gray coating on any part of the plant. It is always unpleasant to come upon an infestation of scale insects: mealy bugs, mites, thrips, black flies, and springtails. These damage the orchid by eating it or sucking its fluids, thereby spreading disease. Then there are snails —with shells or without them—

Scale insects on a leaf.

Red spiders and their web, magnified.

slugs. Their eating habits are annoying, their appetites seemingly insatiable. This is one case where snail pellets are recommended for use prophylactically, whereas other insecticides should always be used for specific problems only.

The number of insecticides offered today is impossible to list. Look to a pest control agent or an orchid dealer for advice and take or send in your leaf and plant samples. Biological sprays and fungicide with insecticide are useful with orchids. Recognizing the problem is half the battle.

Special Types of Orchid Culture

Hydroponic Culture

This type of culture needs no introduction. This is plant care industrial-style—automatic care with seemingly guaranteed success. How deeply this notion is held is revealed in the following experience. Someone brought me a hibiscus in hydroculture. The plant had been losing leaves and its flowers were malformed. It was still blooming but looked sick. What was the matter? The cause was quickly apparent, the plant was nearly covered with aphids.

"Aphids," I said, "look—here, here, there."

"Aphids?—no, that's not right. It can't have aphids—it has been grown hydroponically."

Faith in hydroponics is so widespread that it is no wonder people keep trying to grow orchids hydroponically—sometimes they are successful. Actually the first orchids were grown hydroponically in 1936. But people forget that this approach was employed as a scientific test to try out different fertilizers, and it never was meant to last for any length of time.

We won't go into the fine details of hydroponics but touch upon what is significant for orchid culture. As we have learned, orchids have air roots, thick fleshy ones that have limited powers of adaptation. Therefore, transferring an orchid into a hydroponic setting should always be done before the period of active growth begins. It goes without saying that the plant must first be thoroughly cleaned.

Purchase a hydroponic medium for all epiphytic orchids; terrestrials, such as the lady's slipper, do better in lava.

After transplanting into the hydroponic material that your dealer suggests water normally but don't soak the plant. Use a fungicide prophylactically. Daily spraying with a nitrogen-rich fertilizer will ease the transition. Don't add water until you see the new roots. The water level for all orchids should be about half the maximum. Refill only when the water reaches the minimum level or below. Hydroponically grown orchids are sprayed more frequently.

Hydroponically grown orchids need support and warm water. An electric heating pad of the type used for germination works well. Maintain at 60 to 65° F.

Which orchids are best for hydroponics? In theory, all—but in practice, the monopodial orchids are more successful with the exception of the lady's slipper. Orchids with pseudobulbs must have a rest period without water at a low temperature, or they won't bloom at all. Maintain the same temperature, light, and air circulation, as you would for culture in soil.

Wick Culture

To include all cultivation methods, wick culture will be mentioned here. It has been described as be-

Phalaenopsis in hydroculture.

Caring for Orchids

ing well suited to orchid culture. The theory is that water and nutrients are carried to the orchid by one or more wicks. The potting medium must be capable of holding moisture and transferring it to the plants. Peat, meranti, and other finely textured media are suitable. There is great potential for loss of oxygen within the substratum, with subsequent death of the orchid. Structural stability is maintained by frequent transplanting. The fertilizer solution has to be very weak. All diversions from the usual cultivation in traditional media, at least to date, have been more or less quickly forgotten—among them, Epiflor (bits of styropor that are watered with nutrient-rich fluids), Grolit 2000, or the so called aeroculture (which uses no medium whatsoever). None of these is recommended for the beginner.

Propagation

It doesn't take long before an orchid grower, filled with ambition, thinks about propagating his orchids. It has already been mentioned that this is somewhat more difficult with orchids than it is with other plants. Most of them are propagated by vegetative methods —division of a mature plant. Until the middle of the last century, this was the only means of propagating orchids. This method takes many years to produce large numbers for commercial purposes, but it is the one that most hobby orchidists use. In the following pages, we will discuss it thoroughly.

Division

When is division necessary? (See page 69.) The most common genera, *Cattleya, Cymbidium, Paphiopedilum, Odontoglossum,* and their hybrids don't grow as well after they pass a certain point; they appear to slow down. There are certain situations in which transplanting is indicated, and this is one of them. Although it takes several years for a plant to reach this size, when *Cattleya* are a foot higher than the pot, when *Paphiopedilum* fills a five-liter bucket, and when *Cymbidium* outgrows a 50-liter container, it is time. Perhaps large containers hold too much medium and the plants can't dry out properly. Root

Possible divisions of a sympodial orchid. Only in propagation should fewer than three pseudobulbs be separated from a plant.

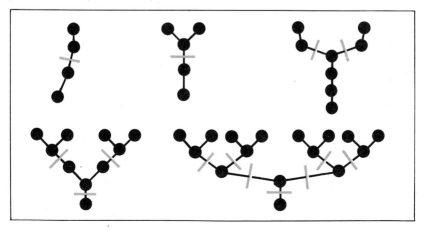

Propagation

growth slows down and with it the rate of growth. But this is only a theory.

Otherwise, an orchid should only be divided when propagation is an absolute must. One good reason might be that the orchid is extremely rare and may be traded, and in such a case you need to decide whether or not the plant is really large enough to be divided. Often a division is necessary when a plant splits into two or more parts by itself (frequently observed in *Paphiopedilum,* but also in orchids with pseudobulbs whose roots have been damaged).

Division of sympodial orchids is relatively easy. Whether only the pseudobulbs or a part of the plant is divided depends upon the size. (See diagram, page 77.) Sympodial orchids with pseudobulbs are treated the same way. Division must always be done with sterile tools (use a flame). Cut places should be allowed to dry out after which they are dusted with charcoal. This procedure is covered in greater detail in the section on transplanting. (See page 66.)

You can begin preparations for transplanting while the plant is still in the container; division proceeds in the places described. Once a cut has been made, place a small piece of styropor in the cut to keep it from growing together. While still in the old pot, the newly divided plant can start a new lead from one of the dormant buds present in all pseudobulbs. This way, when you do transplant, you'll have two or more independent plants to work with. Again, use only sterile tools. Here are a few tips for the more common genera.

- *Paphiopedilum:* The well-known lady's slipper should be handled very carefully. Avoid any tears. When the ball of medium is completely removed, the plant will fall into divisions by itself. Injured leads grow with great difficulty and often die.

- *Cymbidium:* When pseudobulbs are growing tightly together, a division is only possible when the medium is completely removed. Take great care to cause no damage to the pseudobulbs. Use a prophylactic bath of Captan (Orthocide-84) in solution.

- *Cattleya:* It is important not to divide plants of this genus into pieces that are too small. Pseudobulbs with three leaves are the smallest size.

- *Odontoglossum* and relatives: Only divide large plants, or you endanger the potential bloom. All pieces should have well-developed leads.

- *Monopodial:* These orchids cannot be propagated through division. Rooted leads can be cut off like slips *(Vanda, Re-*

nanthera). The lower portion of the plant will easily send out new leads.

Phalaenopsis, like other orchids with pseudobulbs (especially *Dendrobium*), develop plantlets from dormant buds at the plant's nodes. The plantlet will develop roots that will eventually grow large enough to support a separate plant. The little plantlet isn't simply cut off. It is taken with a piece of stem or pseudobulb. The severed places are dusted with charcoal powder. Thereafter it is treated as a young plant.

Development of a plantlet in *Phalaenopsis* (*above*) and on a *Dendrobium* (*below*). Both plantlets have developed sufficient roots to be separated from the main plant. Development of plantlets can often be traced to an error in cultivation.

Propagation

Propagation of Back Bulbs

Sometimes, through division or transplanting, so-called back bulbs, which are generally older ones with no new leads, are left over. They too can be propagated. First remove all remaining roots and potting medium. Any cut places, such as the severed roots should be treated with powdered charcoal. Then pot the pseudobulb in a mixture of sphagnum and styropor or meranti and styropor in a ratio of 1:1.

Choose a pot size that fits the size of the pseudobulb rather snugly, but don't bury it. Warmth will foster development. It also helps to put a plastic bag or glass jar over the back bulb; this heightens the humidity and stimulates growth. The bag or glass should be far enough away to allow for breathing room.

Fresh air is also very important. After several months, when the container is full of roots, you'll have to repot. Carefully loosen the propagation medium from around the roots and repot in "normal" medium, that is, a special orchid mixture.

Tissue Culture

This special method of propagating has extraordinary impact on the practice of horticulture—but for orchid growers it is only important indirectly. Nevertheless, we will describe it briefly here. The concepts of meristem, tissue culture, and cloning come up in every list of orchids. The buyer has to know what is meant by these terms.

In vegetative or seed propagation, there are many genetic possibilities that produce many different and also possibly inferior results. We have already brought up the concept of variety; a variety is normally only propagated through division. But we also know that plants can be propagated by cuttings. Certain types of tissues are capable of regeneration if given a suitable medium—such as the peat and sand mixture for cuttings.

The ultimate number of cuttings obtained from a single plant is

Orchid cultivation *in vitro* (in a flask) in an orchid nursery.

Propagation

limited. Not so in tissue culture, where certain tissues, the so-called meristem tissues, are capable of seemingly endless regeneration when grown in the appropriate medium. The great advantage is that the results are identical. Rare, very valuable, or horticulturally promising orchids can be quickly propagated. This method has only developed in the last two decades and has been made known by the French scientist George Morel. He was able to isolate and propagate the meristem tissue of orchids. That is how we have come to the terms meristem culture and mericloning. Today, other tissue parts are being used as well.

Actual propagation takes place in the sterile conditions of a laboratory. There, a part of the plant is removed and placed on a mixture of agar and other complex nutrients. The nutrient solution is kept in glass tubes or flasks from which the expression *in vitro* comes. The isolated tissue forms a callous, called the protocorm. If it is broken apart, more and more protocorms develop.

This occurs in a liquid medium, which is agitated. Agitation encourages a proliferation of protocorms. When there are enough, they are placed in a solid medium where their cells differentiate and develop into plants.

It isn't surprising that this process takes several months. Not until the plants are well developed are they removed from the flasks and cared

Protocorm before division.

After division the first leaves are discernible. From these leaves new individual plants will grow.

81

Propagation

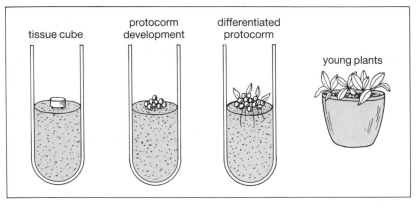

tissue cube   protocorm development   differentiated protocorm   young plants

In tissue culture, small cubes of tissue form the meristem or other tissue parts are removed from a plant. The cubes are placed in a specially mixed liquid medium where they develop into masses of protocorms. These are stimulated to differentiate and develop into new plants. Young plants can later be separated and grown in a special medium.

for as seedlings. (See page 86.) For the orchid collector, a tissue-cultured plant assures that the plant is a clone, identical in every way to the original. The most beautiful and valuable orchids have been reproduced in this manner.

It should be mentioned that chemical or manual injury of tissue under meristem culture in a laboratory can result in mutations. Nevertheless, when you purchase a plant grown from seed, you never really know what you have until it blooms. Other than a few orchids that have been produced en masse like *Vuylstekeara* Cambria 'Plush,' you'll have to pay more for tissue-cultured plants—but you will also be spared disappointment.

Seed Cultivation

We have already mentioned the seed capsule of one orchid (*Vanilla planifolia,* see page 16); the vast numbers and minute size of the seeds have been suggested. Seed development follows fertilization. For the orchid grower, procuring seed is not difficult.

The structure of a flower is well known. Pollen has to be transferred from one flower onto the stigma of another; in the wild, insects do this job. If the gardener wants to fertilize a plant, a swab or wooden stick with a flattened end can be used.

The flower should have been in bloom for several days to be at its prime. The pollen is easy to remove from the anthers and can be pressed lightly on the stigma. The most successful crosses are those of species within a genus, but crossing genera is also possible. The success of a fertilization is difficult to predict; fifty or more tries with hybrids from different genera is not unheard of. But once the plant has been fertilized, the flower will wilt after only a few hours.

After a few days—or even weeks —the column becomes swollen. The pollen tubes penetrate deeply into the cavity where the sperm cells unite with the egg nucleus of an ovule. The actual fusion may

A ripe seed capsule (*Phalaenopsis*) with dust-fine orchid seeds.

take several months in tropical orchids. A capsule is fully ripe when it begins to crack.

Orchids in nature have a symbiotic relationship with different fungi, called mycorrhiza. Expressed more exactly, orchids have an endotrophic mycorrhiza because the fungi penetrates the surface of the root with its hyphae. Ectotrophic mycorrhiza is characterized by fungi that grow between the cells and around the sides of the roots. The presence of fungi encourages the germination of orchid seed. Thus there is more to growing orchids from seed than the simple sowing of seed on a medium.

The individual seed contains an embryo composed of only a few cells with almost no nutritive tissue. Moisture and heat cause the seed to swell and the cells be-

Propagation

gin to divide. Enter mycorrhiza. The fungus penetrates the seed with its hyphae. Within a given capsule, most seeds will not develop because the possibility of the seed's landing on a place where the fungi are growing is slim. The seeds that have the greatest chance of germination are those which land in the vicinity of the mother plant—because that's where the fungus releases a chemical necessary for the development of chlorophyll, which in turn allows for growth. This whole process is much more complex and has been greatly simplified here.

Mature orchids are autotrophic —they are able, with a few exceptions, to live without the fungus. But in nature, the fungus encourages germination. This relationship was discovered at the beginning of the current century. But even before its discovery, there were orchid crosses. How fertilization occurred was known very soon after tropical orchids were imported. But at first, nobody could get the seeds to germinate. It was the observation—or rather the accident—of a seedling in the mother plant's pot that led to the first culture of a young plant. But exactly why this seed had germinated was still a mystery. The orchids were then observed. Soon afterward the first successful orchid hybrid was grown in England.

A suspicion that there was a symbiosis between fungus and orchid existed around the turn of the century, and in 1903 the fungus was isolated.

Symbiotic Method

After isolating the fungus, there was still ground to be covered before the development of a dependable method of propagation. The symbiotic method made use of a sterile growing medium for the culture of the fungus. Once the fungus was present in the medium, the seed would be stimulated to germinate and grow. But at that time it wasn't always easy to keep the fungus pure. Many cultures were infected with other strains that destroyed the seeds.

Asymbiotic Method

In 1922 the revolutionary discovery of the identity of the nutrient the fungus had provided led to a new kind of orchid cultivation. Being able to proceed with an artificial substitute for the fungus was the greatest single breakthrough in orchid culture. With this breakthrough, we return to the laboratory and the growing flask. Similar to the growing media for tissue culture, the seeds are sown on agar enriched with all nutrients necessary for germination. The seeds develop and the young plants are separated in the laboratory.

Propagation

At first, recipes for the growing media necessary to start seeds were heavily guarded secrets; today, you can walk into any store specializing in orchids and buy an instant mix and complete the sowing process in your kitchen. But laboratories are happy to sow the seeds you bring to them. You could also become a real orchid hybridizer.

Don't forget that it's a long way from the sowing of seed to a mature plant. *Phalaenopsis* takes 3 to 4 years, *Cattleya* up to 5 or 6, and lady's slipper may require 8 years.

Above: An asymbiotic seeding of *Phalaenopsis* in a flask. After sowing, the little plants are unevenly thick.

Center: They have to be picked out. They are taken out of the flask and placed in a pot where they have enough room to grow big enough to survive alone.

Below: Phalaenopsis shortly before they were removed from the flask.

Propagation

Caring for Young Plants

Whether plants were started from meristem tissue or seeds, when they come out of the flask, they all require the same care. When they are removed from their glass nursery, they have at least 2 or 3 leaves and their first roots. Their transfer to a no-longer-sterile medium is a critical moment in orchid development. After the old medium is washed off, the little plants are picked out and placed in community pots. The medium should be fine enough to allow these tiny roots to take hold. Flat trays or pots are better, because they dry out more quickly after watering. After separating the plants, they should be treated with a fungicide.

Choose a shady, warm place to keep the little plants. 65 to 70° F promotes optimum growth. Take care when separating the plants not to damage the tiny roots. Plants that are still tangled together after their removal from the flask are of course not simply ripped apart, but carefully separated. Place them in the community pot, lightly touching but far enough away from each other to allow for growth.

Moisture in the medium should be just enough to keep the plants moist but not saturated. Light misting may be all the watering that is needed. Very weak solutions of fertilizer can be given every 14 days. Use a complete fertilizer at the rate of ¼ teaspoon per gallon.

When they are big enough, the plants are again separated. This process may be repeated up to 8 times depending upon genus. Use a single pot when plants approach maturity.

Rather than the usual list of the best-known orchids, this section will concentrate only on those that are available commercially. Hybrids are included with their appropriate genus. The order in which the orchids are listed is in no way meant to be an evaluation—either of popularity or ease of maintenance; it is a simple alphabetic listing.

If many genera currently offered for sale are not mentioned in this section, it is only because of the vast number of available orchids. This book can cover only a small part of the whole. If you are curious to learn more about orchids, there are a number of excellent books and periodicals. Orchid lovers assemble in the American Orchid Society (see page 124). There are a great number of chapters around the country whose members can give practical help and advice. Not to be overlooked are the many orchid nurseries, which not only sell their plants, but offer sound advice as to their care. The kind of thorough grounding in the problems of orchid culture offered here is basic to the care of all orchids.

Aerides

A genus with about 45 species, distributed from India over the Philippines to Japan. A monopodial epiphyte.

Aerides multiflorum Roxb.
Sprays up to 12 inches (30 cm) long, single bloom 1 inch (2 cm) across, pale pink with purple flecks.

Aerides odoratum Lour.
Similar to *A. multiflorum,* but smaller and more fragrant. Hybrids with other genera are known, but not

Flower of *Aerides multiflorum* (shown in half-size).

Orchids from A to Z

very common. Grow in a wooden basket of osmunda fiber. Warm to intermediate temperature. No defined resting period.

Angraecum

A genus with 50 species in Africa and Madagascar (sometimes Asiatic species are included which brings the total of named species to 200). It has become quite rare. No important hybrids.

Angraecum sesquipedale Thou. It is remarkable for its spur, up to 12 inches (30 cm) long on an otherwise white flower. Osmunda fiber is advised. Plants grow quite large with age. A warm house plant. Give little water while resting, good air circulation with an even temperature.

Angraecum sesquipedale; the spur can reach 12 inches (30 cm).

Anguloa

Sometimes described as the tulip orchid, blossoms have a slight resemblance to tulips. A genus with 10 species, seldom offered because it grows very large. Commonly crossed with *Lycaste* (*Angulocaste*). Terrestrial and epiphytic plants originate in the Andes. Intermediate temperature, with defined resting period. Can be grown in any medium. Like *Ly-*

caste, it often drops its leaves in dormancy.

Ascocentrum

A genus with 5 species from the Himalayas and East Indian islands. Epiphyte.

Ascocentrum miniatum Schlechter.
Miniature orchid. Excellent for orchid cases and smaller growing areas. Osmunda fiber. Warm house, no resting stage.

Asocentrum miniatum, a dwarf orchid for room greenhouses and terraria.

mediate temperature. Dormancy. Stems can reach 36 inches (90 cm) long. Not many well-known hybrids.

Bifrenaria

Around 20 species, mostly epiphytes from Brazil to Venezuela.

Bifrenaria harrisoniae (Hook.) Rchb.
This is a plant often recommended for beginners. Successful cultivation is only possible with cool growing conditions. Flowers are yellow-white with attractive purple-veined lips. All growing media. A rest period is absolutely necessary.

Bifrenaria harrisoniae is an easy to grow orchid for cool rooms—if its resting period is observed.

Known hybrids with other genera, *Asocenda* (× *Vanda*), *Mokara* (× *Arachnis* × *Vanda*). Primarily a cut flower. Typical monopodial growth.

Barkeria

15 known species in Mexico and Central America. Epiphytic with long, leafy pseudobulbs.

Barkeria spectabilis Batem.
Pink to violet flowers, easy to grow. Osmunda and other media. Inter-

Orchids from A to Z

Brassavola

This genus, important for every orchid grower, embraces around 15 species. Their distribution ranges from Mexico to Brazil, growing as epiphytes and lithophytes. In order to bloom, all types need bright light. Osmunda fiber is a good medium. Block culture is possible in a greenhouse.

Left: Barkeria skinnerii from Guatemala, easy to grow and bloom. Grows to 20 inches (50 cm) long.

Below: Brassavola nodosa, xerophytic orchid from Mexico, Panama, and Venezuela. At night, blossoms exude a lovely fragrance.

Brassavola nodosa Lindl.
A good subject for intermediate to warm areas. Long, pointed pseudobulbs, around 3½ inches wide, green-white flowers. Heart-shaped lip. This is an easy plant to care for as long as it isn't over-watered. Easily grown in an open window greenhouse.

Brassavola digbyana Lindl.
Now called *Rhyncholaelia,* except for the hybrids that are still *Brassavola.* Remarkable for its fringed lip and its succulent leaves and pseudobulbs. Bright light is important or the leaves will loose their blue-green color.

Brassia verrucosa, the spider orchid; its infloresence can reach 28 inches long. A single flower can be almost 6 inches across. Many crosses have been made with *Brassavola,* especially with *B. digbyana,* for its fringed lip.

B. × *Cattleya = Brassocattleya*
B. × *Cattleya* × *Laelia = Brasso-laeliocattleya*
B. × *Cattleya* × *Laelia* × *Sop-hronites = Potinara*

Unfortunately, *Brassocattleya* are hard to come by. Because of their large leaves, they are considered old fashioned in the garden industry. Their cultivation is the same as *Cattleya.* Respect their resting stage.

Brassia

There are 35 epiphytic species from tropical America. The common name "Spider Orchid" comes from its flower. All growing media are possible. Intermediate temperature, good air circulation, resting period important, cultivation easy.

Brassia verucosa Lindl.
Green-gold sepals, petals are flecked black. Easy to grow, fertilize lightly, respect its resting period. In the last few years, Brassia crosses have been available. Unfortunately, the blooming

period leaves something to be desired.

B. × *Miltonia* = *Miltassia*
B. × *Odontoglossum* = *Odonto-brassia*
B. × *Oncidium* = *Brassidium*

Cattleya

One of the most beautiful of all genera (45 named species, all epiphytic) hails from Central and South America. Crosses from this genus belong in every orchid collection. Only the most important species will be named here. All are recommended. Grow using instructions for *Cattleya* hybrids which are given in detail.

Cattleya bowringiana Veitch.
Cattleya dowiana Batem.
Cattleya intermedia Grah.
Cattleya labiata Lindl.
Cattleya loddisgesii Lindl.
Cattleya mossiae Hook.
Cattleya skinnerii Batem.
Cattleya trianae Lindl.

Of all *Cattleya, C. labiata* has played the most important role of all in breeding. Its discovery was made by an English traveler and collector of mosses and lichens. His name was William Swainson. He found plants in the Brazilian Organ Mountains and, not recognizing the orchids, used them as packing material. One of this explorer's packages was sent to the first true orchid collector in the

Cattleya hybrid, the so-called "Semi-alba" type (half-white).

A *Cattleya* hybrid of typical form and color.

Orchids from A to Z

Laeliocattleya 'Princess Margret,' a named variety (F.C.C./R.H.S.).

The exception to this rule is *C. dowiana* and its hybrids (these are the large-flowered yellow *Cattleya*) which have to be kept warmer. Any growing medium may be used, as long as good drainage is maintained. Setting buds occurs right after the resting period in most *Cattleya* species. Exceptions to this rule are the summer blooming *Cattleya*, which may begin to bloom when the shoots are only half grown. *Cattleya*, like all orchids, are transplanted independent of season, when active growth begins.

A remarkable feature of the *Cattleya* is the sheath that grows from the top of the pseudobulbs, in which flower buds develop. Once in a while, a sheath doesn't form —sometimes not even during the growth period, and then reappears the next year. Such plants may bloom without a sheath. Often a sticky, sugary coating collects on the sheath, a trap for ants that carry aphids along with them.

In the course of its development, the sheath can turn from light

modern sense, one William Cattley. Luckily, he preserved the packing material and grew it in his greenhouse. In November 1818 the first glorious *Cattleya* bloomed. Of course, at first it wasn't called that. It was John Lindley who first described it and named it *"Cattleya"* to honor Cattley.

Behind the seemingly dry plant names, are many exciting stories that make working with this family of plants even more fascinating. Later on, more *C. labiata* were found, and now many varieties are common in collections.

As far as the cultivation of these orchids is concerned, all need intermediate growing conditions.

Cattleya guttata from Brazil. Unfortunately its bulbs grow a yard long.

green into shades of brown or even black. This is perfectly normal. In indoor grown plants that bloom in winter and spring it can be avoided by simply cutting the sheath off. Once in a while buds get stuck in the sheath, and this calls for cautious action. It is best to hold the sheath up against the light in order to see the buds clearly and avoid damage to them.

Cattleya shouldn't be allowed to keep growing—something they are prone to if given a warm position. After the lead has hardened, water must be reduced and the temperature lowered to about 50 to 55° F.

Cattleya pseudobulbs grow fibrous tissue to protect them from the light. This sheath shouldn't be removed, but it should be watched so that mealy bugs or scale insects don't harbor there. Of the many *Cattleya* hybrids, here are some of the most important ones:

C. × Laelia = Laeliocattleya
C. × Sophronites = Sophrocattleya
C. × Laelia × Sophronites =
　　　Sophrolaeliocattleya
C. × Epidendrum = Epicattleya

Cattleya hybrid developed from the yellow *C. dowiana.*

Orchids from A to Z

Chysis

There are only 6 known species of this genus, unfortunately they are only rarely cultivated. They come from Mexico, Colombia, and Venezuela. They require intermediate temperature, a defined period of rest, and an osmunda medium. For their very long pseudobulbs growth in a wooden basket is recommended. Flower spikes hang down.

Cirrhopetalum

This genus will only be mentioned here because the warm temperature species are excellent for orchid cases. Grow on bark; it requires little medium. All species have small blossoms.

Coelogyne

This is a species hailing from the southern slopes of the Himalayas. There are almost 200 known species from all temperature ranges. If you buy one, find out where it came from. Use osmunda. Wooden baskets are good. *C. cristata* Lindl. Striking, almost round pseudobulbs, pure white, relatively large flowers with a gold comb on the lip. A well-known orchid for cool conditions. Maintain its rest period faithfully. Fern fiber and wooden baskets make excellent containers. It may bloom on lightly shrunken pseudobulbs during the rest period. Hybrids within the genus are rarely available.

Cymbidium

Coming from tropical Asia and Australia, this is a commercially important genus with about 40 species. Their long-lasting blooms and their excellent growth characteristics are the reasons for their popularity. Flower shops will carry both the single blossoms and the inflorescences. There are about a dozen species under cultivation for cut flowers.

Because the plants grow very big, they are not practical as houseplants. These are plants for greenhouses and conservatories. They are divided into large-flowered hybrids and miniatures.

Coelogyne cristata from the Himalayas. This species, brought to Europe in 1837, has been grown since then.

Orchids from A to Z

Here we will describe the culture of a very popular hybrid. The standard *Cymbidium* hybrids need a cool, bright (only shade in summer), and very airy situation. They belong to a group of orchids that are half terrestrial and half epiphytic, but perform beautifully in any available peat-based medium. They have no defined resting period, but should be kept a bit drier after they bloom. In spring and summer, the temperature should go no lower than 55°F. Days can be substantially higher, but never over 95°F. In summer they need abundant water and fertilizer. On hot days, spray them and allow for fresh air. A half-shady place in the garden will take care of their needs.

They are divided into early, middle-, and late-blooming types. The early ones will need their high day temperatures lowered at night. This temperature difference stimulates the formation of buds. If the night temperatures do not drop, the plants won't form buds. This is the main problem with growing *Cymbidium:* It is difficult to induce bloom in home conditions. *Cymbidium* hybrids need heavy fertilizing but must be protected from a buildup of salts in their containers. Let water run through their medium several times in summer to flush out salts. Red spider is the pest to watch out for. Immediate recognition and action is important. In winter, the plants need a temperature of 50 to 55°F; higher temperatures can cause the buds to drop off.

Miniature *Cymbidium* hybrid 'Show Girl' is suitable for home growing.

Miniature *Cymbidium* hybrid 'Mary Pinchess' is a relatively large plant approaching standard *Cymbidium* in size, but easy to bring into bloom.

Hobby orchidists should choose plants that induce bloom in the high day and low night temperatures of their homes. *Cymbidium* don't tolerate transplanting well; choose a structurally stable medium and restrict transplanting to only once every 4 or 5 years. They do well in large containers. As has been mentioned, standard *Cymbidium* grow very large. Within the genus, hybridizers have bred smaller species that sometimes diminished flower size as well. The miniature *Cymbidium* are better pot plants. When crossed with species requiring warm temperature they may suit our home conditions even better. In 1960 miniature *Cymbidium* cultivation took a great leap forward when it was crossed with the species *C. pumilum* Rolfe. So decisive was that cross that now when you hear people talking

Orchids from A to Z

about miniature *Cymbidium*, they will call them only *Cymbidium pumilum.*

This species blooms in early fall and its descendants bloom early and are easily induced. Grow like the standard hybrids with a slightly warmer temperature.

Dendrobium 'Lady Hamilton.'

Dendrobium

The genus *Dendrobium* belongs to the orchid most richly endowed with species; there are more than 900 of them. The name indicates an epiphytic life-style—something like "living (bios) on a tree (dendron)." It is not possible to name which among these species is the most important. Even their distribution is immense—from Korea and Japan over the Malaysian islands to Indonesia, Australia, and New Zealand. There are *Dendrobium* for every temperature range; ask about their origin when purchasing.

Hybrids are also numerous. We often see the cool growing *Dendrobium nobile* hybrids. They come from *D. nobile* Lindl., which has to be overwintered at 50°F. This species has the tendency to drop leaves formed in the previous year during its resting phase before the flowers appear on the leads. Without a rest period, no blooms will develop.

The descendants of *D. phalaenopsis* are handled very differently; they won't survive without a warm temperature and are not recommended for home growing. These are important cut flowers, imported from Asia by the millions. Their long-lasting flowers make them very popular.

Dendrobium loddigesii (shown actual size), a dwarf form for intermediate temperatures. If their rest period is maintained, they bloom easily.

The intermediate temperature is necessary to grow many *Dendrobium* including dwarf forms like *D. loddigesii* Rolfe. and others. Wooden baskets or bark culture works well with all species; osmunda is the medium of preference. Many *Dendrobium* grow plantlets —generally an indication of an error in cultivation—but these very plantlets allow *Dendrobium* to be easily propagated.

Encyclia

From Florida over to Mexico to Brazil, 130 species of this genus are to be found. After the genera were redefined, we have found many members previously listed as *Epidendrum* among the *Encyclia*. Hybrids are listed under *Epidendrum.* All species require intermediate temperatures. They need good light and fresh air. Use os-

Orchids from A to Z

munda with smaller species, peat or similar media with larger ones. Almost all species have an extremely long period of bloom.

Epidendrum

Grow as *Encyclia*. This is a genus with over 1,000 species; crosses with *Cattleya* and *Laelia* are common.

Laelia

Not all orchids are named for those who had something to do with the plant's discovery. This genus is named for a Roman, Gaius Laelius, who distinguished himself in the third Punic War, about 14 BC. Exactly why Lindley chose to honor this officer is not known. The genus has around 60 species divided into two geographic areas. One is the area of Mexico and Central America; the other is northern South America to Brazil and Peru. Similar to the *Cattleya*. This genus is often crossed with them.

All *Laelia*, even the very small ones, have bright colors—red, orange, and yellow. Many grow epiphytically, a few terrestrially or even lithophytically. Cultivation is similar to that of *Cattleya*, but the kinds with thin almost round leaves and pseudobulbs need more light. In addition, they need good fresh air and air circulation. All lithophytes need a definite resting stage with cool temperatures, during which they should not be allowed to dry out completely. The orange-red color of *Laelia* has always enticed hybridizers. Many *Cattleya* hybrids with small blossoms, but excellent durability were the result. Only two important species will be included, both from Brazil. These are highly recom-

Laelia pumila comes from Brazil; never allow its medium to dry out completely.

Left: Encyclia vitellina, better known as *Epidendrum vitellinum*. It requires cool temperature and has a long-lasting flower.

Laelia purpurata, the national flower of Brazil, with its very attractive shape and distinguishing lip color.

among the rare orchids. The older crosses that retain the *Laelia* character are recommended. Grow like *Cattleya* hybrids.

L. × *Cattleya* = *Laeliocattleya*
L. × *Brassavola* = *Brassolaelia*
For other hybrids, see *Cattleya.*

Lycaste

Lindley took this name from antiquity as well—the name of King Priam's lovely daughter. Forty species are found from Mexico to Brazil, and both epiphytes and terrestrials are among them. They only carry their leaves for one season. They must have their resting phase observed with low temperatures down to 42° F, during which time they should be very nearly dry.

Lycaste skinnerii Lindl.
This best-known species from the mountain regions needs a cool temperature and won't grow well in the home although it is always recommended. Frequently, hybrids are seen in England.

mended for a collection in an intermediate temperature.

Laelia pumila Rchb.
The most beautiful miniature orchid has 4-inch blossoms with a striking purple lip. Grow them in wooden baskets with osmunda and the roots will have adequate air. Use organic fertilizers.

Laelia purpurata Lindl.
This species with giant, mostly white flowers and purple lips, has stolen the heart of every orchid lover. Numerous varieties with carmine or almost blue lips are still

Masdevallia

There are around 200 known species, and lately many new ones have been discovered. They grow in the mountains up to 12,000 feet in high humidity—but not in cloud forests. They come from the mountains of tropical Central and South America. At first glance, their flowers seem atypical of orchids, being tube-shaped with a small lip. Grow them in cool temperatures and high humidity, but allow for fresh air. They are easiest to grow in special collections and are among the most interesting orchids of all. *Masdevallia* hybrids are very seldom lost.

Masdevallia triangularis comes from Venezuela. In winter, keep the temperature above 50°F.

Maxillaria

This genus with over 300 species is found in vast areas of Central and South America. It is easy to grow in intermediate temperatures and almost any medium. It has been crossed with *Lycaste* to produce insignificant but interesting blossoms.

Lycaste skinnerii; a new synonym is *Lycaste virginalis.* It is the national flower of Guatemala where it is called "Monja Blanca," and frequently found on coins and postage stamps.

Orchids from A to Z

Miltonia

This genus with around 25 species comes from Brazil, Colombia, Costa Rica, and Paraguay. The Colombian hybrids are of particular interest. They need an intermediate climate with a shady situation and fresh air.

The growth period begins in the fall months, the best time to transplant. They should never be transplanted in the summer because only plants with healthy, intact roots live through the summer heat without injury. Use meranti or a mixed medium composed of ⅓ osmunda, ⅓ sphagnum, and ⅓ styropor. *Miltonia* are very sensitive to salt and need little fertilizing.

During root development (of untransplanted specimens) there are often difficulties. As soon as the root tips reach the surface of the

Top right: Miltonia hybrid 'Celle,' a modern hybrid for intermediate temperatures.

Below right: Miltonia 'Bluntii,' a hybrid of *M. spectablis × M. clowesii,* both Brazilian species where *M.* 'Bluntii' was found as a naturally occurring hybrid.

Left: Masdevallia coccinea comes from Colombia and Peru, where they are found at heights of 7,000 to 8,000 feet.

Orchids from A to Z

medium, which may be of salt-retaining plastic, they burn. This can be prevented if a layer of sphagnum is used on top of the peat. Then, when the roots reach the top, they will turn toward the interior of the container.

The flowers last for several weeks or more, as long as they remain on the plants. There have been numerous crosses in the last few years, with other genera as well.

M. × Brassia = Miltassia

M. × Brassia × Cochlioda × Odontoglossum = Beallara

M. × Cochlioda × Odontoglossum = Vuylstekeara

M. × Oncidium = Miltonidium

M. × Odontoglossum × Oncidium = Colmanara

Odontoglossum

The renaming of this genus, a relative of *Miltonia,* has caused much confusion among gardeners and scientists in the last few years. Well-known species, like *Odontoglossum grande,* were included in the genus *Rossioglossum.* Because this plant is still called by its former name in some quarters, we have left it in its former genus. There are many hybrids.

The 200 species of this genus are similar in origin. They usually come from mountainous areas between 4,500 and 10,000 feet above sea level. They are found in a wide area, covering Central America with an area of higher concentration in the Colombian Andes.

Vuylstekeara Edna 'Stamperland,' hybrid grown in 1921.

Typical *Odontoglossum crispum* hybrid 'Stern von Kolumbien.'

Odontioda 'Coronation,' an old cross from the Belgian hybridizer, Vuylsteke, after whom *Vuylstekeara* is named.

Odontioda are genus hybrids of *Odontoglossum × Cochlioda.* The most important *Odontoglossum* species is *O. crispum* Lindl. Its fabulous flowers can grow to 3½ inches across on a multiflowered inflorescence. Their color is white to whitish pink and they are called 'Stern von Kolumbien' (Star of Colombia). One plant of *O. crispum*

Their origins determine their cultivation: fresh air, low temperatures. Most of the hybrids, however, can be grown in intermediate temperatures in the home. All media are useful but have to be of good structural stability to allow for adequate air supplies in the root zone. Among the straight species, there are a few which are hardy. *Odontoglossum* species are grown in cool temperatures in the greenhouse or conservatory.

Hybrids may be divided into two groups. One is treated like *Odontioda* whereas the other needs the same conditions as *Oncidium.*

Odontoglossum pulchellum, the fragrant May bell orchid from Mexico and San Salvador.

Orchids from A to Z

was sold for more money than any other orchid. They are not well suited to home cultivation because of the low temperatures they require. The most striking colored hybrids of all orchids are found among the *Odontioda*—from red to yellow, lilac to brown—anything is possible. High humidity is necessary.

These hybrids were crossed with another genus that tolerates higher temperatures, *Oncidium. Odontoglossum × Cochlioda × Oncidium = Wilsonara,* and *Odontoglossum × Oncidium = Odotocidium.* These hybrids are handled like those of Miltonia. *Odontoglossum × Cochlioda × Miltonia = Vuylstekeara.*

It is especially important to observe the phases of growth of all of these plants, because frequently —about every 8 months—they can stop growing and begin to bloom. The resting period may show up at any part of the year—in the middle of summer or in spring. All hybrids are suited for home cultivation and surprisingly adaptable to different temperatures. When growth begins, they can be transplanted, although summer months should be avoided (like *Miltonia*). Choose a container that isn't too large but allows the plants to dry out once in a while.

Above: Wilsonara 'Pimlico.'

Right: Oncidium kramerianum.

Oncidium

In the genus we find over 500 species; no other genus has such variety. *Oncidium* orchids are suited to all temperature ranges. Make sure, when you purchase one, to check its origin. Because the genus *Odontoglossum* is similar, as already described, there are many crosses. Among the straight species, osmunda as a medium is preferred, although hybrids will grow in any suitable medium. Use organic fertilizers.

Orchids from A to Z

Succulent leaves are a sign of a bright situation: Their main flower color is yellow. Many species stay small and are suitable for orchid cases. Crosses with *Oncidium* should be handled like *Odontoglossum*.

Paphiopedilum

The genus of the famous lady's slipper includes 60 species. Their importance in the orchid family is supported by the numerous hybrids. And their long-lasting cut flowers have made them commercially important.

The genus *Paphiopedilum* belongs only to the Asian forms. All other lady's slippers including the native one, belong to other genera. Even so, there are *Paphiopedilum* from all temperature ranges—cool, intermediate, and warm. Their area of origin reaches from South India to the Himalayas, from China to Southeast Asia. Nearly all are terrestrial with thick, widespread roots which should be accommodated in the appropriate container. Among the species, *P. callosum* turns up frequently as a pot plant. Thailand is its country of origin. It requires warm temperatures and is easy to grow in the home. Earlier, species from the Himalayas were attempted but were only suitable for very cool rooms. The new hybrids are generally from warm growing species; they are easy to grow.

Paphiopedilum species have no means of storing nutrients and must be kept moist and fed throughout the year. But you still have to watch for the beginning of growth. The medium for *Paphiopedilum* should hold water well. Peaty media are well suited. But don't forget the addition of lime. Their light needs are not particularly high, especially in summer when they need shading. Every lead blooms only once, but should be maintained so that the area that photosynthesizes is greater. Only

Right: Paphiopedilum callosum.

Left: Modern *Paphiopedilum* hybrids.

Orchids from A to Z

divide very large plants. (See page 78.)

Because it will be some time before they are tissue-cultured, vegetative propagation is necessary. Very attractive hybrids are quite expensive. For home cultivation, some of the multiflowered species are suitable. Always ask when purchasing which temperatures the plant needs.

Phalaenopsis 'Fischers Liebling,' an older cross with flowers like the straight species. Today, large round flowers are preferred.

Left: Two blossoms of *Phalaenopsis* 'Schoene von Celle,' a modern hybrid grown for cut flowers. *Right:* The original species of white *Phalaenopsis, Phal. amabilis.* It was a long way, over several generations, from one to the other.

Phalaenopsis

The genus *Phalaenopsis* includes 40 species from India, Malaysia, New Guinea, and northern Australia. No other orchid has enjoyed a similar surge of popularity as a houseplant. This is due to its uncomplicated adaptation to warm rooms.

The plants of this genus, like those of *Paphiopedilum*, have no means of storing nutrients and must be regularly cared for. They grow monopodially and have wide, fleshy leaves. Flowers come in various sizes but are always long-lasting.

There are thousands of hybrids in all colors from white to lilac to yellow. They need semishade in summer and as much light as possible in winter or the buds drop. Any medium is suitable. They respond to fertilizing. Air roots that grow over the pot should not be injured. Thus the inflorescence should be removed for safety's sake or the plant will exhaust itself. *Phalaenopsis* often sends out a second inflorescence. Cut this back so that 2 to 3 nodes remain on the stalk. A new flower stalk will almost always grow from these nodes. Sometimes, instead of flowers, a plantlet develops, often a sign of cultivation mispractice such as overwatering. Nevertheless, as soon as roots develop, make cuts above and below it along the stalk and plant. The portions of stalk will decompose over time. Never tear the plantlet from the stalk.

117

Orchids from A to Z

These species are easy to grow in the manner previously described. If the flowers are generally smaller, they have retained their original attraction. Through crosses of these species with large-flowered hybrids, the so-called "star type" came about—star-shaped in contrast to the often round flower forms found in this genus. Often dots or stripes show up on the petals, delighting their growers. Crosses with other genera are seldom undertaken because they grow slowly and bloom poorly. An exception is the genus *Doritis: P. × Doritis = Doritaenopsis.*

Crosses from these genera tolerate low temperatures and often have intense colors.

From top to bottom: The *Phalaenopsis* variety, 'Golden Sands,' *'Ambotris' (Phal. amboinensis × Phal. equestris),* and 'Munsterlandstern' belong to the star types. They and similar crosses are grown as pot plants, but are not suitable for cut-flower growing. A warm room (70° F) is desirable.

Sophronites

All 7 species of this genus are well known and all are from Brazil. Most important is *Sophronites coccinea* Rchb., which was introduced as a genus hybrid with the *Cattleya*. It has bright red flowers and belongs to the dwarf orchids. Grow in osmunda in an intermediate temperature. Use organic fertilizer and keep the plant evenly moist, but not wet.

Stanhopea

Generally these are epiphytic plants with about 25 species in all tropical regions of South America. Their hallmark is their short-lived but very large flower. All are very fragrant.

Stanhopea tigrina Batem. The best-known species comes from a large area stretching from Mexico to Brazil. *Stanhopea* should be grown in a wooden basket because its flowers hang, forming clusters. In winter, the night temperature should be no lower than 50° F. In summer, keep them in the open.

Sophronites coccinea. "Sophron" means "modest"; here it refers only to the size of the plant—not the flowers.

Orchids from A to Z

Vanda

60 species belong to the genus *Vanda*, one that, unfortunately, is seldom successfully grown in the home. Cut flowers of amazing durability are most often imported. The home of this genus is in tropical Asia, in the Philippines, in the Malaysian archipelago, in Australia, and in New Guinea. All need warm temperatures, a bright situation, and high humidity. Use a small amount of medium; grow in a wooden basket where the plant can remain for a few years. Water and feed over the numerous air roots rather than over the medium. The blue color of the blossoms of some species like *Vanda coerulea* adds to the attraction of its culture.

Left: Stanhopea tigrina, an interesting orchid with a short lived flower.

Below: Vanda tricolor comes from Java and Laos. The Indian name from the first description has been retained.

Orchids from A to Z

Zygopetalum brachypetalum has a habit similar to the better-known *Z. mackayi* or *Z. intermedium.* It is found in the mountains of Brazil.

Zygopetalum

Blue is a color seldom seen among orchids. It is no wonder that the mostly blue flowers of *Zygopetalum* hybrids are highly prized, even though the genus hasn't been used for much hybridizing. There are around 30 known species, mainly epiphytic. They originate in Brazil, Paraguay, Argentina, Peru, and Bolivia. They are middle-sized plants that develop their flowers along with the new lead. The roots of most species are especially thick and numerous. A large container is always necessary. All media are suitable and good air circulation is desirable. Fertilize during the period of active growth. Flowers are only produced if the plant is kept cool enough (in winter not below 55°F). Flowers last for several weeks. In summer, place in semishade, out in the open with plenty of fresh air.

Further Information

American Orchid Society
6000 South Olive Avenue
West Palm Beach, Florida 33405

Office Manager: Marguerite
McDonald

The AOS can provide information
about local chapters. It also
publishes the "AOS Bulletin."

Index

Index

Index

Other Macmillan Gardening Guides are available
at your local bookstore or from
Macmillan Publishing Company

To order directly, mail the form below to:
MACMILLAN PUBLISHING COMPANY
Special Sales Department
866 Third Avenue
New York, NY 10022

	Quantity	ISBN	Title	Price	Total
1	_____	0020626606	**Bonsai**	$6.95	_____
2	_____	0020635206	**Orchids**	$6.95	_____
3	_____	0020633602	**Berry Gardening**	$6.95	_____
4	_____	0020631308	**Ornamental Gardening**	$6.95	_____
5	_____	0020631502	**Organic Gardening**	$6.95	_____
6	_____	0020631405	**Natural Herb Gardening**	$6.95	_____

Please add postage and handling costs—$1.00 for the first book and
50¢ for each additional book—and applicable state sales tax.

TOTAL $ _____

_____ Enclosed is my check/money order payable to Macmillan Publishing Co.

_____ Bill my _____ MasterCard _____ Visa Card #_____

Expiration date _____ Signature _____
—Charge orders valid only with signature—

	Lines	Units

Control No. _____   T–Code _____   _____

Account Number/San _____   For charge orders only:

Ship to: _____   Bill To: _____

_____   _____

_____   _____

_____ Zip Code   _____ Zip Code

For information regarding bulk purchases please write to Special Sales Director at the above
address. Publisher's prices are subject to change without notice. Offer good January 1,
1986 through December 31, 1986. Allow 3 weeks for delivery.

FC#274